Frances A. Shaw

A Brief History of Russia

Third Edition

Frances A. Shaw

A Brief History of Russia
Third Edition

ISBN/EAN: 9783337170615

Printed in Europe, USA, Canada, Australia, Japan

Cover: Foto ©ninafisch / pixelio.de

More available books at **www.hansebooks.com**

THE EASTERN QUESTION.

A BRIEF

HISTORY OF RUSSIA,

FROM THE SMALL BEGINNINGS OF THE NATION
TO THE PRESENT VAST PROPORTIONS
OF THE EMPIRE;

WITH ACCOUNTS OF THE SUCCESSIVE DYNASTIES.

BY

FRANCES A. SHAW.

𝔚𝔦𝔱𝔥 𝔐𝔞𝔭𝔰.

THIRD EDITION.

BOSTON:
JAMES R. OSGOOD AND COMPANY,
Late Ticknor & Fields, and Fields, Osgood, & Co.
1877.

Copyright, 1877,
By JAMES R. OSGOOD & CO.

FRANKLIN PRESS:
RAND, AVERY, AND COMPANY,
BOSTON.

SOVEREIGNS OF RUSSIA.

		PAGE.
1.	Oleg, 879–912	6
2.	Igor, 912–945	7
3.	Queen Olga, 945–957	8
4.	Sviatoslav, 957–972	8
5.	Vladimir the Great, 980–1015	9
6.	Jaroslav, 1026–1054	11
7.	Vladimir II. (Monomachus), 1113–1126	12
8.	Mstislas, 1126–1132	14
9.	Alexander-Nevsky, 1252–1262	15
10.	Ivan III. (The Great), 1462–1505	15
11	Vassili III., 1505–1533	18
12.	Helena	19
13.	Ivan the Terrible, 1533–1584	20
14.	Feodor, 1584–1598	30
15.	Godunof, 1598–1604	31
16.	Dmitri the Impostor, 1605	32

17. Vassili Shuiski, 1606–1610 46
18. Michael Romanoff, 1613–1645 47
19. Alexis, 1645–1676 48
20. Feodor III., 1676–1682 49
21. Peter the Great, 1689–1725 52
22. Catherine, 1725–1727 61
23. Peter II., 1727–1730 67
24. Anna, 1730–1740 68
25. Elizabeth, 1741–1762 69
26. Peter III., 1762 70
27. Catherine the Great, 1762–1796 . . . 71
28. Paul I., 1796–1801 81
29. Alexander I., 1801–1825 84
30. Nicholas I., 1825–1855 100
31. Alexander II., 1855– 115

A Brief History of Russia.

Russia, that giant empire, which is of so comparatively recent a date that its past seems but a day in the annals of Europe, has a history cruel and sanguinary indeed, but full of thrilling and wonderful events.

With an area of more than eight million square miles, it clasps four seas, and one-third of Europe and Asia, in its far-reaching arms, and contains a population of nearly ninety million souls, of widely diverse races and customs, yet all so united as to form one homogeneous whole. For two and a half centuries Russia was under Tartar rule; and to this day it unites the two totally unlike civilizations of the Orient and the Occident.

The earliest known inhabitants of Russia were the Scythians in the south, the Slavonians in the interior, and the Finns toward the north. To these three great nations belonged many smaller tribes; and among them were the Russ, or Rossani, from whom the country takes its name.

Before the ninth century, Novgorod, a republic lying near the Gulf of Finland, had risen to great prominence; and its capital city of the same name, "the republican mother of a despotic empire," had become so powerful that it was a common saying among the people, "Who dare oppose God and Novgorod the Great?"

But dissension arose, foreign invasion threatened, and assistance was asked of Rurik, a noted Varangian chief. It proved such assistance as might have been expected of an ambitious and unscrupulous warrior. Rurik repelled the invaders, overawed the rebellious factions, made himself master of the country, and laid broad and deep the foundations of the Russian Empire. After a reign of fifteen years, signalized by conquests and victories, Rurik died, leaving the government to his infant son Igor, Oleg, his kinsman, being appointed regent.

OLEG, 879-912.

Oleg lived but for the aggrandizement of his country; and he was entirely unscrupulous in regard to the means employed in securing this, the one purpose of his heart. As Kief had a milder climate and was farther advanced in civilization than Novgorod, he resolved to make it his capital; and, under pretence of desiring to treat with its two princes, he drew them into an ambuscade, and had them put to death.

Exulting in the success of his nefarious deed, "Let Kief henceforth be the mother of all Russian cities," he said; and it remained for three and a half centuries the capital of the empire.

IGOR, 912-945.

Oleg reigned thirty-three years, and left the government, enlarged and consolidated, to Igor, who seems never to have complained, though he was nearly forty years of age when he succeeded to his father's throne. He was a well-meaning though inefficient sovereign; but his wife, Olga, a woman of more than ordinary talent and ambition, ruled her husband while he lived, and at his death became regent, and guardian of their young son and heir.

QUEEN OLGA, 945-957,

is a favorite subject of old Russian romance and ballad literature. She is represented as having been a very beautiful peasant-girl, whom Igor met while travelling through the country in disguise, and married, without disclosing his true rank.

The first of Russian sovereigns to renounce Paganism, she publicly embraced Christianity at Constantinople, and received baptism, the Greek emperor and empress acting as her sponsors. A grand entertainment followed the interesting ceremony, the table at which Olga and her sponsors sat being of solid gold.

Olga tried to introduce the Greek ritual among her people, but her efforts were unavailing. They were wedded to the old superstitions, and to them Perune, the chief of Russian deities, was more than the God of the Bible.

SVIATOSLAV, 957-972.

Sviatoslav, the heir to the throne, to his mother's great sorrow remained true to the Pagan deities of his ancestors; but he was a chivalrous, valiant prince, the idol of his army, whose dangers and privations he shared, faring in all respects like the humblest soldier of the ranks. As sovereign he won a name in war and conquest, and left Russia larger and more powerful than he found it. At his death, the realm was divided among his three sons, who fought for the supremacy, until, in 980, Vladimir, the youngest, gained sole dominion.

VLADIMIR THE GREAT, 980-1015.

On the day of his baptism into the Greek Church, Vladimir received the name of Basilius; and, if we may credit the Russian annals, twenty thousand of his subjects were baptized on the same day with him.

As a reward for his acceptance of the new faith, Vladimir received in marriage Anne, the sister of the Greek emperor. Russia henceforth belonged to the patriarchate of Constantinople, and Kief became the nursing mother of the still feeble church, just transplanted to a foreign and uncongenial soil.

Under this reign, the idols of Paganism were destroyed, churches were built, learning and the arts were cultivated, and Russia was raised to the highest pitch of Gothic glory. "Sunny Prince Vladimir" and his valiant deeds for centuries remained a favorite theme for minstrelsy; and his epoch is considered the heroic age of Russian history.

Historians, recognizing the superiority of Vladimir to the rude age in which he lived, have surnamed him "the Great;" and the names of both Olga and Vladimir Basilius stand high on the Greek calendar of saints.

But the sunlight of impartial truth must too often dispel the poetic nimbus which romance and tradition throw around the heroes and heroines, the saints, even, of the past; and sober history tells us that Saint Olga, though far in advance of her time, was a woman who could be both cruel and revengeful; that Saint Vladimir, with all his rude greatness and many chivalric qualities, was a fratricide and a polygamist.

At his death, in 1015, Vladimir committed the fatal error of dividing the empire among his seven sons. His example being followed by subsequent rulers, the history of Russia until the fifteenth century is a record of anarchy and bloodshed.

"In thus dividing his empire," says the historian Müller, "Vladimir the Great retarded the advancement of commerce and letters, diminished the political importance of Russia, and replunged its people into the barbarism from which they were just beginning to emerge."

After long and sanguinary warfare among the rival brothers and their partisans, Jaroslav and Mstislas, in 1026, jointly assumed the government, and ruled amicably for ten years, when Mstislas died, leaving his brother sole sovereign of this shapeless and colossal empire.

JAROSLAV, 1026-1054,

in Russian annals is honored with the surname of "the Wise." He gave the first code of laws to his country; and Russia reveres in him not only a wise legislator, but an enlightened and merciful sovereign. He established schools; and, though he fostered the Greek Church, he allowed no religious persecution. He caused the Holy Scriptures to be translated into the Slavonic tongue, transcribing several copies with his own hand.

He was a politic prince, and strengthened his

government by brilliant matrimonial alliances. His sister became Queen of Poland; his three daughters, queens of Norway, France, and Hungary; while his daughters-in-law were Greek, German, and English princesses.

This sovereign, so wise and far-seeing in all else, at his death, after a reign of thirty-five years, partitioned the empire among his five sons, who fought against one another, and, dying, bequeathed the unnatural strife to their descendants.

VLADIMIR II. (Monomachus), 1113-1126.

Jaroslav died in 1054, and, during the next hundred and eighty years, seventeen princes sat upon the throne, among all of whom we find but one truly great man, Vladimir Monomachus, who was crowned in 1114. Amid the darkness and barbarism of his age he stands forth a colossal figure, the tutelary genius of Russia. He waged no wars but those the safety of his country demanded; and, though his heroism on the field was never called in question, it was by deeds of moral heroism that he won his fairest laurels.

Upon the character of this great and good sovereign there rests no stain. On his death-bed he wrote out a brief record of his life, interspersed with much good advice, and many wise maxims for his children. A few of these maxims will suffice as an index to the character and policy of this just man : —

"Be fathers to the orphan, be yourselves judges for the widow. Put to death neither the innocent nor the guilty; for nothing is more sacred than the life and soul of a Christian. My dear children, praise God and love men. It is neither fasting, nor solitude, nor monastic vows, that can give you eternal life : it is beneficence alone."

Not being in the direct line of succession, Monomachus twice refused the crown bequeathed to him by the dying king Vszevolod, and urged upon him by the almost unanimous voice of the people ; and he only accepted it at last to save his country from fratricidal strife and ruin. He reigned thirteen years ; and so great was his popularity at home and abroad, that the Greek emperor sent him the ensigns of the imperial dignity, — a golden tiara set with diamonds, a cross and sceptre of gold, with other costly gifts, as a token that he considered the Russian prince his equal.

MSTISLAS, 1126-1132.

The first wife of Monomachus was Gyda, daughter of Harold, the last Saxon king of England. Mstislas, the son of this marriage, succeeded to the throne. He inherited the virtues of both parents, and, in his too brief reign of six years, carried out the wise, pacific policy of his father. After his death, chaos came again to Russia. In the course of thirty-two years, eleven princes grasped the sceptre, each holding it only until another more powerful wrested it from his hand.

The Poles, taking advantage of the distracted state of affairs, invaded the empire which the Tartars, under Ghengis Khan, at length subdued. During the two and a half centuries of Russia's subjection to the Tartar yoke, its sovereigns held their domains only as appanages from the khan, to whom they were compelled to make occasional journeys, consuming a year's time, in order that they might humbly sue for the right of governing. On these visits they were treated in the most insulting manner, being allowed to present their petitions to the khan only when prostrate on the ground at his feet. The Tartars also exacted large tribute, under conditions most galling to the national pride.

ALEXANDER-NEVSKY, 1252-1262.

From the time of the first Tartar invasion, in 1237, until the accession of Ivan III., in 1462, Russian history is a chaos of uncertainties and traditions, through which looms up the figure of one great and good sovereign, — Alexander-Nevsky. He drove back the Swedes, the Germans, and the Lithuanians, who flung themselves upon the tottering empire; he made three weary journeys to Asia to conciliate the khan, who had it in his power at any moment to crush the already humiliated and conquered nation. On his return from the last journey he died, a martyr to his patriotic zeal. The Russian Greek Church has made a saint of him. Would that all her canonized ones were as worthy!

IVAN III. (The Great), 1462-1505.

Before the accession of Ivan III., who was of the line of Rurik, and is surnamed "The Great," many causes had been at work, tending toward the liberation of Russia from her degrading Tartar servitude; but it was this sovereign who at last threw off the detested yoke. Ivan III. was the first of Russian emperors to assume the title of Czar, — not a corruption of Cæsar, as some have supposed, but a word from the Persian, signifying supreme authority.

For his second wife Ivan married Sophia, the daughter of Constantine, the last Greek emperor. When Byzantium fell into the hands of the Turks, this princess had sought refuge within the sacred walls of Rome; and the Pope had not turned a deaf ear to Ivan's entreaties that she might share his Muscovite throne. This exalted alliance confirmed his autocracy, and enabled him to place upon his ensigns the two-headed eagle, type of supreme power. With this august Greek princess, the luxurious customs of the Orient, the forms and ceremonies of the Byzantine court, the arts of Greece and Rome, were introduced into Russia. The haughty Sophia could ill brook the idea of having her husband a vassal of the khan, and compelled to submit to his humiliating exactions. She gave the czar no peace until he had thrown off the galling yoke.

Ivan III. was a haughty, ambitious prince, who sought to raise his throne to an equality with the proudest in Europe. Fearing lest the sovereigns of older and more enlightened nations might regard him as a *parvenu*, he stood very much upon his dignity, compelling all who would have dealings with him to treat him as an equal. He instructed his ambassador at the Turkish court neither to bend the knee to the Sultan, nor to yield precedence to any other ambassador. He refused one daughter to the King of the Romans, and regarded the marriage of another to the Margrave of Baden as very much beneath his dignity.

This barbaric Louis XIV. was a most strenuous advocate of the divine right of kings. He declared that he had received his throne from the high and mighty Trinity, and would not degrade himself by accepting titles from any prince on earth. During a long and prosperous reign he did much to enhance the material greatness of the nation. By the promise of liberal rewards, he enticed skilful artificers from abroad. He built the Kremlin, and adorned it with all the splendors of barbaric art: many other stately edifices also rose at his bidding in his capital of Moscow, to which the seat of government had been removed in the fourteenth century.

He caused cannon to be made, and adopted their use in his armies with great success; he had the mines worked, and silver and copper money coined in his own capital; he established intercourse with foreign nations, and first rent the veil which separated Russia from the rest of Europe.

Ivan's era was one of pomp and show, of gorgeous pageants and entertainments, of Oriental forms and ceremonies; but there was no moral element in all this grandeur, nothing that could promote the best interests of the people.

Though personally accused of cowardice, Ivan III., through his armies, won some splendid victories. During his long reign of forty-three years, nineteen thousand square miles were added to the territory of Russia, and four million souls to its population.

VASSILI III, 1505-1533.

Ivan's grandson by his first marriage was heir to the throne; but the haughty autocrat said to his boyars, "I will give Russia to whom I think proper, and I command you to obey." So, consigning his grandson to perpetual imprisonment, he chose for his successor Vassili, the son of the Czarina Sophia, who, at his father's death, assumed the sceptre without the least opposition. Ivan III. died in 1506, at the age of sixty-seven; and, four years after, the captivity of the true heir, Dmitri, ended in a violent death. Vassili strictly followed the policy of his father, and, after a reign of twenty-eight years, left the empire, enlarged and strengthened, to his infant son Ivan, Helena his wife being appointed regent.

HELENA,

the second female sovereign of Russia, — Olga being the first, — was a woman of depraved character, and entirely under the influence of a favorite corrupt as herself. When, after six years of crime and misrule, Helena died, none regretted her; and no inquiries were instituted as to the cause of her death, though it was supposed to have been from poison.

IVAN THE TERRIBLE, 1533-1584.

The government was now in the hands of a council of regency, with Prince Andrew Shuiski at its head. Shuiski and his associates were unprincipled, designing men, who in every way sought to corrupt and brutalize the young czarowitch, and thus render him incapable of reigning.

Terrible deeds of cruelty were enacted before his very eyes; and, if the lad chanced to show favor to any one around him, the life of that favored one was instantly in danger.

His guardians mocked at his better impulses, and applauded his crimes. When he tortured young animals, or, in his furious drives around Moscow, trampled old people and little children under his horses' hoofs, they commended him as if he had done some brave and chivalrous deed. They treated his friends with the greatest indignity; and even he, the descendant of so long a line of sovereigns, was often the object of abuse and contumely. These men seemed to delight in visiting on this helpless heir to the throne the insults they had received from his mother the regent Helena.

Under such pupilage, all that was good in Ivan's nature was repressed, all that was bad was stimulated and fostered. He reached his fourteenth year, old in wickedness, and ripe for revolt against his tormentors and oppressors. He declared that he would rule without the aid of a council, and, in a momentary fit of rage against Andrew Shuiski, ordered him to be thrown to his dogs.

"They have well deserved the repast," he said.

The order was obeyed, and by this horrible death the head of the powerful house of Shuiski expiated a life of violence and crime. But the Gluiski, another powerful family, now rose to ascendency in the state, and exerted a no less baleful influence upon the czarowitch.

In his eighteenth year, after a minority of blood and horror, Ivan was crowned czar. His atrocities were so great, that the long-suffering people at length, driven to desperation, fired Moscow in several places at dead of night.

Ivan awoke amid flame and smoke and the imprecations of the populace. At this very moment, one Sylvester, a monk who pretended to divine inspiration, appeared before the young czar with an open gospel in one hand, and the other raised in the attitude of prophecy. He warned Ivan of the wrath of Heaven, which was even now visiting his evil deeds, adducing certain signs which had recently appeared in the sky as tokens of the anger of an offended God. Alexis Adashef, the one good man among all Ivan's evil counsellors, seconded the monk in his efforts at reforming the czar; but their most powerful ally was Anastasia, Ivan's beautiful young bride, a princess of the Romanoff family, a woman of the most sweet and gentle disposition, and possessed of a mind superior to the age in which she lived.

Religious fervor and love combined wrought an entire change in Ivan's character. He became almost a fanatic in his new-born zeal: when he took the city of Kazan from the Tartars, he changed the mosques into Christian temples, and compelled the khan to be baptized. He showed himself, also, a progressive sovereign, and sincerely desirous of the good of his people.

But the tiger in his nature was only slumbering to awake ere long into tenfold fury. The beneficent influence of Anastasia and Adashef lasted thirteen years, and all the greatness and glory of Ivan's long reign of half a century are comprised within this brief period.

Anastasia died. Ivan, who was just recovering from an illness which is supposed to have partially crazed his brain, was haunted by an unjust suspicion that she had been poisoned, and sought to revenge her death on all his subjects. From this time, suspicion and terror constantly brooded over his darkened soul: he distrusted all who approached him, and lived in momentary fear of assassination.

The mad atrocities of his career after Anastasia's death can be explained only on the ground of insanity. These atrocities surpass belief, and form the most sickening page of Russian history. There those who have a taste for horrors can find them in full detail. In comparison with Ivan IV., justly called in Russian annals "Ivan the Terrible," Caligula and Nero become almost respectable.

One of his most stupendous crimes, and yet it was but one among many, was the destruction of Novgorod, the mother of Russian cities, — a commonwealth older than Florence, and much larger than the London of that day. It was a city rich in historic memories, and linked with the whole past of Russia, whose capital it had been six centuries before the Kremlin was built at Moscow, ten centuries before St. Petersburg rose on the banks of the Neva. There may even now be found in the Kremlin a bronze group, typifying its reign of a thousand years.

A proud, a wealthy, a luxurious city, its walls embraced a circuit of fifty miles, and it contained four hundred thousand souls. This city, "Novgorod the Great," had offended Ivan by its love of liberty, its wealth and independence, but, above all, by its hatred of his rule, and its efforts to be taken under the protection of Sweden.

He swore that he would raze Novgorod, and sow its site with salt; and, invading it with an army of thirty thousand Tartars, he raged there for six weeks like an infuriated tiger. His orders to his soldiers were, "Burn, slay, give no quarter to old or young!" With his own hand he aided in the wholesale butchery. The streets ran blood, the river was choked with the bodies of the slain. His victims numbered sixty thousand.

The greater part of the city was pillaged and burned. Novgorod never recovered from the catastrophe: it is now an insignificant city.

Other smaller cities shared the same fate; and in Moscow, his own capital, he enacted scenes of horror too terrible for description. Often, at the closing act of one of his greatest atrocities, he would say, piously lifting his eyes to heaven, "My dear people, I ask an interest in your prayers."

One of Ivan's martyrs was Philip Prior, a priest of great purity of heart and life, who had dared rebuke the crimes of the czar to his very face. The Greek Church has canonized Philip. His remains have been removed to Moscow; and on the day of his coronation every czar of Russia must kneel before his shrine, and kiss his feet.

"Ivan the Terrible" violated all law, human and divine. In defiance of the strictest canons of his church, he had a plurality of wives. When already the husband of seven living wives, he aspired to the hand of Queen Elizabeth of England. As that obdurate maiden would not listen to his suit, he made a formal offer of his heart and hand to one of her ladies of honor, Mary

Hastings, daughter of the Earl of Huntington. But the Lady Mary, though at first dazzled with the prospect of a throne, concluded to decline the dangerous and doubtful honor; and nothing remained to the discomfited wooer but to soothe his lacerated affections by putting to death the ambassador through whom his matrimonial overtures to the English court had been made.

No sovereign has ever been so great an enigma to historians as Ivan IV. If he was mad, there was certainly method in his madness. To him Russia owes its complete deliverance from Tartar rule. His conquests were many and valuable, and in them all he supplanted the crescent by the cross. Although personally a coward, his arms proved more than a match for the Swedes and the Poles. He opened Russia to foreign trade, introduced printing, reformed the clergy, assembled a parliament to consult upon the common weal, and drew up a code of laws in many respects admirable. Always terrible to the rich and great, he was often a benefactor of the poor. It has been said that there were in Ivan two distinct beings, — the great man and the wild beast.

"I am your god, as God is mine," was his

common declaration to his subjects. He would walk about the streets of Moscow, ordering this one to be beaten, that one to be put to death. No age, sex, or condition was exempt from his fury. In a fit of frenzy he killed with a single blow of his iron staff the only one of his three sons who was fit to rule, and he was ever after consumed by an undying regret: of remorse he was incapable. He died soon after, in 1584, having reigned fifty years, twenty-six of which were one unintermittent fever of fury and revenge.

"How could the people suffer such a monster to live and reign?" we ask, as we read the record of Ivan's appalling crimes; and we find our answer in the character of the Russian people. Nowhere is the sentiment of loyalty so deeply rooted as in Russia; nowhere is "that divinity which doth hedge a king" so sacred. The uneducated masses of Russia, even in our day, can imagine no limitation to the power of the Czar. "I believe in God in heaven, and the Czar on earth," is an article of the creed, which, even so late as the reign of the Emperor Nicholas, they taught their children.

Amid all the horrors enacted by Ivan, the people looked upon him as their anointed sovereign, God's vicegerent, who had power over life and death, who alone could preserve the purity of the national religion, and save millions of souls from endless perdition. When sometimes, in his frenzies of passion, he would threaten to leave his throne, they would most abjectly entreat him to remain, offering their lives as a sacrifice to his righteous anger, if such should be his sovereign will and pleasure.

The Russians of this period, though sunken in the deepest ignorance, imagined themselves the best informed people on earth; but among them astronomy, anatomy, and kindred sciences, were regarded as diabolical arts; the learning of their priests was confined mostly to a little Latin and less Greek; their only mode of reckoning was by means of balls strung upon strings, and the skins of wild beasts had just ceased to be their current money. Reading and writing were occult mysteries confined to the learned few.

For ages Russia had been ground down by a twofold despotism, — that of the sovereign and that of the Greek Church; later, to these was added the savage Asiatic despotism of the Tartars. And yet this nation of slaves bore the yoke uncomplainingly, believing it to have been imposed by God.

A father in his thatched hut was as despotic as the czar on his throne: he had power over the lives of his children, he could sell them into slavery. Russian wives had less freedom than their Asiatic sisters, and were treated with great barbarity. Prisoners of war were slaves; insolvent debtors were given to their creditors; the poor man could sell himself to the rich man.

Slaves must imbibe the vices of their enslavers, and the Russian character of this day exhibits traces of its vile Tartar servitude. National pride and personal honor were crushed out of the Russian heart, and cunning and greed had usurped their place. With the Tartars came the knout and all sorts of corporal punishments. The manners and customs of the people were borrowed from the Greeks as well as the Tartars, and showed generally the worst traits of both. Every individual of a family was involved in the ruin of one of its members. To leave the country was rebellion and treason: there was no asylum from the all-prevailing despotism of the czar. Always in danger from civil war and outside invasion, the natural ferocity of both prince and people was aggravated by fear.

FEODOR, 1584-1598.

Ivan IV., dying, committed his eldest son and heir to the guardianship of the Council of Boyars, at the head of which was his brother-in-law, Boris Godunof. This son, Feodor, though old enough to assume the sceptre, was weak both in body and mind; a harmless imbecile, whose greatest pleasure from early childhood had been to hide away in the church-towers, and ring the bells.

Boris Godunof knew that while Feodor lived he could remain supreme in power, and that at his death (an event which could not be long delayed) he might, were it not for one obstacle that stood in his way, assume the title of Czar. This obstacle was a boy of ten years, Dmitri, the son of the seventh wife of Ivan IV.

On the afternoon of May 15, 1591, this lad Dmitri, who is represented as a mad, ferocious little imp, was found with his throat cut in the courtyard of the royal palace at Uglitch, where he lived with his mother, the dowager Czarina Mary. As Boris alone had interest in the death of the czarowitch, he was generally supposed to have instigated the murder. Seven years after, Feodor, the last male representative of the line of Rurik, died. This house had reigned nearly eight centuries, and had given fifty-two sovereigns to the empire.

GODUNOF, 1598-1604.

Boris attained the summit of his ambition: he was crowned Czar of Russia. He ruled with an iron hand, and so insulated the throne by the terror of his name and deeds, that, though remote branches of the line of Rurik still existed, none dared aspire to the sovereignty. He exiled the great princes whom he could not cajole or coerce, and he won over the petty nobles by chaining down the wandering peasantry to the soil. Of Tartar descent, and fully imbued with the savage spirit of Asiatic despotism, Boris Godunof was just the man to oppress Russia with the heavy yoke of serfdom at a time when bondage to the soil had ceased in the rest of Europe.

The administration of Boris was brilliant and

able. Under his rule, Russia won a name both in diplomacy and arms; but, though respected abroad, the czar was feared and hated at home. The noblest and best families were in exile. Crushed under the heel of a ruthless despotism, the people had become sad and sullen. Joy was dead, and a dim, brooding horror had usurped its place. The minstrels who had been wont to traverse the land were seen no more: their songs of war and love and chivalry, once so dear to high and low, were heard no longer.

The Cossack peasantry, an industrious, peaceable race, fled in a body from the tyranny of Boris, taking refuge among their native steppes of Asia; and a horrible famine of three years' duration spread mourning and despair over the whole country.

DMITRI THE IMPOSTOR, 1605.

While the disasters of Russia were at their height, a report spread among the people, that it was a peasant-child, and not the czarowitch, who had been murdered; that Dmitri was still living in Poland.

The rise and fall of this false Dmitri form

one of the most romantic episodes of Russian history. His real name was Gregory Otrepief; and he was a young monk who could both read and write. These accomplishments, rare at that day, had won him a place in the service of a Polish prince, who passed much time at the court of the czar. It is related, we know not how truly, that this prince one day gave his secretary a box on the ear, and that the youth immediately burst into tears, saying, "If you knew who I am, you would not treat me so." He then told a very plausible story, declaring that he was Dmitri, the true heir to the Russian throne. The story seems not to have made much impression upon the Polish prince at the time, but he afterwards espoused the impostor's cause.

From some old servants of the Czarina Mary, Otrepief learned many particulars in the life of the murdered czarowitch. He also ascertained the names and titles of the officers who had been attached to the boy's person, and by some means obtained possession of a seal bearing Dmitri's initials, and a cross set with diamonds, said to have been his baptismal gift.

Having well studied and prepared his part, he

begged permission to retire to his cloister. When asked how he could leave the court, where, with his talent and learning, a brilliant future might be in store for him, he replied, laughing, "By remaining here I should become a bishop, at the highest; but I mean to be Czar of Russia."

This frequent declaration having reached the ears of Boris, he gave orders to have the crazy monk sent to a remote cloister, and thought no more about him. Otrepief set out under the escort of two monks, whom on the journey he won over to his side, persuading them to accompany him to Lithuania, where the czar had many open enemies. Whenever they tarried for the night at a wayside monastery, Otrepief would write on the wall, "I am Dmitri, son of Ivan IV. Although believed to be dead, I escaped from my assassins. When I am upon my father's throne, I will recompense the generous men who now show me hospitality."

Far and near the people caught up the tidings that the true heir was yet alive. The young monk was now twenty-two, — the age Dmitri would have been, if living. Those who had known the Czar Ivan in his youth fancied that

Otrepief resembled him in form and feature, while his dark complexion and reddish hair were those of the Czarina Mary. Like Dmitri, he had one arm longer than the other, and two warts on the face, — one on the forehead, the other under the right eye. These marks of identity, together with the royal seal and the diamond cross, were regarded as ample proof that the young man was not an impostor.

Many believed in the genuineness of his claims; and very many, at heart incredulous, espoused his cause from motives of policy, or hatred to Boris Godunof. The Jesuits became his most zealous supporters, and the Pope's nuncio promised the aid of the sovereign pontiff, if Otrepief would promise, when he became czar, to further the interest of the Latin Church. Hatred to Russia alone would have made Sigismund, King of Poland, a willing ally of the impostor, had there not been other and stronger reasons for espousing his cause. The Cossacks of the Don flocked to the pretender's standard. The Ukraine declared for him, and he soon raised an army of fifteen thousand men, with which he appeared on the Russian frontier. Boris had already sent a force of fifty thousand against him. After some fruitless skirmishing, the decisive battle was fought on the 20th of January, 1605.

Just before entering the fight, Dmitri stood in front of his army, and prayed fervently, committing his righteous cause to the God of battles. He then addressed his soldiers, so exciting their enthusiasm by his glowing eloquence, that all resolved to conquer, or die with their leader. The issue of the contest was for a long time doubtful; but the impostor remained master of the field.

So profound a policy seemed to dictate all his actions, that many suppose him to have been a close student of Machiavelli. For reasons best known to himself, he was in no haste to enter Moscow and seize the crown, — that glittering prize which for three years had been the sole object of his dreams, and which was now just within his grasp.

In a manifesto issued soon after his victory, he said, "Let Boris Godunof descend from the throne he has usurped, and in the solitude of the cloister seek to make his peace with Heaven. In that case I will forgive his crimes, and assure him of my protection."

Boris well knew that the Czarowitch Dmitri had been murdered by his express command; but, tortured by remorse for his many crimes, he fancied that the avenger of blood was upon his track. The phantom of his youthful victim was ever before his diseased imagination: he believed that the son of Ivan IV. had really risen from his grave, and headed the victorious army that was about to enter Moscow and drive him from his throne.

The autocrat trembled with fear; but he gave no outward sign. His court, one of the most splendid in Europe, remained gorgeous as ever: he still sat at the council board, and directed the affairs of the empire.

All this time he was plotting suicide; but he resolved to die as he had lived, — a sovereign. Just after rising from a splendid banquet, given to some distinguished foreigners in the " gilded hall " of his palace, he was taken alarmingly ill, and in two hours expired. None doubted that his death was caused by poison, administered by his own hand.

His son Feodor, a youth of sixteen, whom he had named as his successor, reigned just six weeks, and then, with his mother and sister Xenia, was cast into prison. Dmitri (for so we must call him) treated the royal captives with respect and kindness; but six years after, in the next reign, Feodor was strangled.

On the 20th of June, 1605, the impostor made his triumphal entry into Moscow, and was crowned in the palace of the czars. The people were wild with joy: this Dmitri, whoever he might be, had found a way to all their hearts. Possessed of a commanding and agreeable person, and a persuasive eloquence, he was gracious and affable in manner, and yet dignified as became a sovereign. The brilliancy of his intellect seemed equalled only by the goodness of his heart.

Just after his coronation, the false Dmitri, in sight of an admiring multitude, knelt in tears before the tomb of Ivan IV., and, kissing the stone with well-feigned transport, cried, "O father! thy orphan reigns; and this he owes to thy holy prayers." His emotion was contagious. All wept with him.

The opening of his reign was auspicious. He surprised his ministers by his thorough acquaintance with the empire, its wants and resources, by his prodigious memory, and his rare executive ability. He set about reforming abuses, and showed himself a man who would have neither favorite nor master. On both public and private occasions he laid aside the usual solemn etiquette of the czars, and was always easy of approach. Every Sunday and Wednesday he appeared at the threshold of his palace to listen to the grievances of the people, and receive their petitions with his own hand. The good of his subjects appeared to be the one great wish of his heart.

He was so humane and moderate in the use of victory, that those who believed him an impostor began to wish he had really been born to the purple. "I have sworn not to shed Christian blood," he said; "and I will keep my oath. There are two ways of governing an empire, — by tyranny and by generosity. I choose the latter. I will not be a tyrant."

Dmitri had been a month in Moscow, and, to the great surprise of all, he had not yet seen his mother. At last it became noised abroad that the royal nun was about to quit the convent where Boris Godunof had compelled her to retire; that she was advancing to Moscow. Dmitri went out to meet her, and, in a sumptuous tent which had been erected at Toininsk, he welcomed the widow of Ivan IV. They were for a little time alone, probably arranging the part they were to act; then they came out of the tent, and embraced with every token of the liveliest affection. Dmitri had said to the czarina, "You can have in me a good son or a severe master;" and here, in the presence of all the people, she acknowledged the impostor as her son.

The young czar led his alleged mother to the carriage which was to convey her to Moscow, and walked beside it bareheaded the greater portion of the way. He assigned her apartments in the Kremlin until he could have a magnificent palace built for her, and allowed her a household and a revenue befitting the mother of the czar. He visited her every day, and treated her with the most unbounded respect and affection; even consulting her upon affairs of state, and joining her name with his in the ukases he issued. The most incredulous began to believe that this was really the czarina's son.

The new czar still devoted himself with patient assiduity to the affairs of his empire, forming many schemes for reform at home, and aggrandizement abroad. But his popularity was on the wane. His attachment to the Poles (the hereditary enemies of Russia), his preference for the Latin Church, his open contempt for Russian ignorance and for Russian manners, proved most disastrous to him, and at length wrought his ruin.

During his stay in Poland, Otrepief had fallen in love with Marina, the young and beautiful daughter of the Palatine of Sendomir, and the father had given his consent to the marriage after the youthful wooer should become czar.

The czar summoned his betrothed to Moscow. She came, attended by her parents and relatives and a numerous Polish retinue. On the 18th of May, 1606, the marriage was celebrated with great pomp. The Poles of the bride's retinue, however, bore themselves in the most arrogant and insulting manner towards the Russians, and the old, undying animosity was kindled anew.

A sullen discontent reigned among the people. The czar had already surrounded himself with Polish counsellors and favorites; he had derided the old Russian traditions and customs, and, though nominally an adherent of the Greek Church, was more than suspected of being a Papist at heart. But the greatest sin of all was this marriage with an unbaptized woman, — the Greek Church baptizes only by immersion, — a Polish heretic.

Discontent rose to fury, when some evil-minded individuals circulated a report that the czar's body-guard, all Polish soldiers, in order to terrify the Russians with the power of the new sovereign, were about to begin an indiscriminate massacre among the populace. The clergy went from house to house, calling on all true sons of the Church to rise and avenge the insults their faith had received from the heretic Dmitri and his Polish allies.

Prince Vassili Shuiski was the leader of the rebellion. He had before headed a conspiracy against the new czar, and had been sentenced to Siberia. But Dmitri with his usual good-nature had pardoned his bitterest and most powerful enemy, and even given him a place in the councils of the empire.

At daybreak on the 24th of May, the whole city was in open rebellion. Dmitri was warned of his danger, but he would not listen. "I hold Moscow and the empire in the hollow of my hand," he said, and laughed at the fears of the officers of the guard.

"Orthodox Christians," shouted Shuiski, "death to the heretic!" Thousands of voices took up the cry, "Death to the heretic!" The great bell was rung, and the three thousand bells of Moscow answered it. The houses where the Poles lodged had been marked with chalk; and the Russians, bursting open the doors, began to massacre the slumbering inmates.

The palace of the czar was stormed by an armed mob, shouting, "Death to the impostor!" Dmitri seized a sword, and defended himself with great bravery. He is said to have slain several of the conspirators with his own hand. The guards, also, defended their master to the last, many losing their lives in a vain effort to save him. Finding resistance useless, Dmitri at length leaped from a back-window of the palace, and in the fall broke his leg. Fainting with pain, he was seized by the infuriated mob, his groans being answered only by jeers and insults. He was not put to death at once, as his assassins wished to prolong his sufferings. His imperial robes were torn from him, and he was invested with the caftan of a pastry-cook.

"Look at the czar of all the Russias!" shouted the mob: "he has now put on the dress which best befits him."

"Dog of a bastard!" cried one of the nobles, "tell us who you are, and whence you come."

Dmitri replied firmly and distinctly, —

"Every one of you knows that I am your czar, the legitimate son of Ivan IV."

"Monk Otrepief," said Prince Shuiski, "confess yourself an impostor, that God, before whom you are shortly to appear, may have mercy on your soul."

"I am the Czar Dmitri," replied Otrepief, still unwavering. "This is not the first time that rebellious subjects, led astray by traitors, have dared lay hands on the sacred person of their sovereign; but such crimes never go unpunished."

And with this falsehood on his lips he died, shot through the heart by a Russian merchant named Valuief, who, forcing his way through the mob, cried, "Why talk so long with this accursed heretic? This is the way I'll shrive the Polish piper!"

Otrepief's death was the signal for a general massacre of the Poles. "Down with the Pope! death to the heretics!" was the cry. For six hours the streets of Moscow ran blood, and more than a thousand Poles were slain. Marina and her father, concealed by some friendly Russians, escaped amid the general confusion; but they were afterwards imprisoned, and kept in close confinement for years. After a life of many vicissitudes, Marina ended her days in prison.

The body of the impostor was burned, and his ashes were scattered to the four winds. But new Dmitris were to rise from those ashes. Rumors that Dmitri was not dead, that he had escaped in the tumult, that the mutilated body exhibited as his to the populace was not that of the czar, became rife in the land. Four swift horses were missing from the imperial stables, and it was currently reported that three horsemen in Russian costume, but speaking Polish, had been ferried across the Okra. One of them had given the ferryman six ducats, saying, "You have ferried the czar: when he returns to Moscow with a

Polish army, he will not fail to requite the service." Encouraged by the success of the first impostor, several other pretenders to the throne appeared, each claiming to be the true Dmitri. All were in time silenced, though not without much bloodshed.

VASSILI SHUISKI, 1606-1610.

Vassili Shuiski succeeded Otrepief as czar; but, after a stormy reign of four years, he was deposed, and cast into prison, where he ended his days. One great noble after another grasped the sceptre, only to be deposed, perhaps put to death, by a more powerful rival, for none of these princes ever dreamed of showing mercy to a fallen foe. It was a period of anarchy and civil warfare, during which the patriotism and resolution of the clergy alone prevented the utter ruin of Russia.

THE DYNASTY OF THE ROMANOFFS.

In November, 1612, the throne being vacant, the Boyars met in council, and despatched letters to every town in the empire, summoning the clergy, nobility, and citizens to send delegates at once to Moscow, with full power to meet in the national assembly, and proceed to the election of a czar. A fast of three days was appointed, that the people might invoke God's blessing on the choice of a new sovereign. This fast was most religiously observed throughout the land.

MICHAEL ROMANOFF, 1513-1645.

The day of election came: it was in Lent of the year 1613. The choice at length fell upon Michael Romanoff, a youth of sixteen, personally unknown, but recommended by the virtues of his father, a high dignitary of the Greek Church. The Romanoffs, a family long distinguished for brilliant public service and exalted patriotism, were, through the female branch, connected with the royal line of Rurik.

Before assuming the crown, Michael bound himself by the most solemn oaths to protect the Greek Church, to seek no revenge for injuries done his family, to change none of the old laws, to make no new ones, to declare neither war nor peace, to decide upon nothing without the advice and consent of his council, to surrender his own estates, and incorporate them with the domains of the crown.

The land was once more at peace; pretenders to the throne no longer appeared; old feuds were healed; diplomatic relations were formed with other countries; and Russia began to take her place among the nations of Europe. During Michael's long reign, his object was peace rather than glory: his era was one of convalescence for Russia, wasted by so many years of war and tyranny. He was the founder of the present powerful dynasty of Romanoff.

ALEXIS, 1645-1676.

There have been but two dynasties in Russia, — that of Rurik, and that of the Romanoffs. Michael, the founder of the second dynasty, ruled wisely and well, although his reign was not brilliant, for thirty-two years, and then died, leaving the empire to his son Alexis, who, during a reign of thirty-one years, proved so humane, sagacious, and successful a prince, that he is often called in Russian annals, "the Father of his Country." He formed an alliance with Poland against Gustavus Adolphus, neither country being able to cope singly with the veterans of the Thirty-Years' War. The Swedish king was at length forced to submit to terms of peace; Russia, as a reward for her assistance, receiving vast accessions of territory from Poland.

Alexis promoted learning and the arts; but his efforts to introduce into Russia the customs of more enlightened nations met with but slight success. Russia had been Asiatic under the Ruriks: the Romanoffs sought to make it European, but progress was slow. The people, who were grossly ignorant, were wedded to the old customs and superstitions. Ere long, in Peter the Great was to arise a master-mind, who would civilize them, even against their will.

FEODOR III., 1676-1682.

Feodor, the son of Alexis, who succeeded to the throne at nineteen years of age, was a prince weak in body, but strong in mind. He instituted many reforms, which his early death prevented being fully carried out. His aim was internal improvement rather than outside conquest. The pride of the nobles had become insufferable, the family which could show the longest genealogical record being the most arrogant. Feodor, under pretence of correcting certain errors in these records, ordered them to be brought to court. He then convoked an assembly of the highest civic and clerical dignitaries of the realm, and, in an eloquent harangue, set forth the dissensions of which the records were so constant a source, and advised that they should be burned, the names and dignities of the noble families being first inscribed in a set of books opened for that purpose. The desired assent was given. The records, being heaped up in the courtyard of the palace, were set on fire; and with them perished the ridiculous assumptions of the old nobility of Russia.

In accordance with Oriental custom, the czar had long been in the habit of choosing his consort from among his own people. On an appointed day, the worthiest and most beautiful young girls from the noble families were invited to the imperial palace, that the czar might select a wife from among them. They came in most gorgeous apparel, and were entertained with great festivities, lasting often for days. During all this time, the prince critically and attentively watched every movement of the young ladies, even listening secretly to their most private conversation. At length, having made his choice, he seated himself at table with his young guests, and there presented the favored one with a handkerchief and a ring, dismissing the rejected damsels with rich gifts. His choice was then declared in public, the future czarina receiving the title of crown princess. Alexis had chosen two wives in this manner.

Feodor, having witnessed the bitter feud between the two rival families into which his father had married, resolved to choose a wife of another nation. As he had already formed an ardent attachment to a Polish lady, inclination as well as principle led to this decision. The Church uttered its anathemas in vain: the young czar married the lady of his love. When, after a too brief reign of six years, Feodor died, "Moscow," says a Russian chronicler, "was plunged into as deep mourning as Rome at the death of Titus." Feodor left no heir. Himself the son of Alexis' first marriage, he had six own sisters, and one own brother, Ivan. As Ivan was imbecile, Feodor chose his half-brother, Peter, the son of his father's second wife, Natalia, as his successor.

PETER THE GREAT, 1689-1725.

The family of the first wife resolved to retain the succession; and Sophia, the eldest daughter of Alexis, a princess of great beauty and talent, united with a courage equal to any emergency, contested the crown, first in the name of her idiot brother, then in her own. The Naryskines, the family of the second wife, were equally active in pressing the claims of Peter, then a boy ten years old.

Sophia at length gained over the Strelitz (National Guard), and let them loose on the adherents of Peter. A carnage of three days ensued, during which the two brothers of Natalia, and sixty of her kindred, were cruelly massacred. Natalia fled from the capital, taking with her the boy Peter. It is said that for sixty wersts she carried him in her arms, the Strelitz following close upon her path. Her strength began to fail; and, in her terror and despair, she rushed into the convent of the Holy Trinity for sanctuary. She had just time to reach the altar, and place the child upon it, when, with yells of savage triumph, the murderous band entered the convent. One of them seized the boy, and was about to cut off his head, when the sound of horses' hoofs was heard outside. The frightened ruffians fled; and PETER THE GREAT was preserved to Russia.

Ivan was declared sovereign; but, idiotic though he was, he had sense enough to know his unfitness to rule, and begged that Peter might be associated with him. The request was granted; and on the 6th of May, 1681, Ivan and Peter were crowned czars, Sophia being chosen regent on account of the imbecility of the one, and the youth of the other. Sophia, being now seated on the throne, began to take steps toward retaining it. Her first proceeding was the banishment of her brother, in his tender years, to an obscure village, where she gave him a guard of fifty profligate young men, hoping that evil associations would so debase him in body and mind as to render him unfit to reign. The vices of Peter's life — and they were many — may be ascribed to these corrupting influences: his virtues were his own.

There were talent, education, and honor even, among these debased young men. Belonging to Peter's guard was a Lieutenant Timmermann, who gave him lessons in military science and mathematics: there was also a certain Lefort, a Genoese, of depraved morals, but a man who knew the world, and had been a close student of social life and of books. He had seen much diplomatic service, had mastered several languages, and, with all his faults, cherished a sincere friendship for Peter. He acted as the young czar's tutor; and years after, when Peter had risen to the summit of power and greatness, Lefort became his most valued counsellor. He organized a military company of the fifty young men, and here Peter took his first lessons in the art of war. His mental abilities were of the highest order, and his advancement in all his studies was unusually rapid. While Sophia believed that her brother was becoming unfitted to rule, he was actually rising superior to the wild, bacchanalian life around him, and preparing himself to act his part as one of the most able and well-informed of sovereigns.

As Sophia was about to assert the claims of a false heir to the throne, — the reputed son of the imbecile Ivan, for whom she had negotiated a marriage, — Peter, at his mother's solicitation, married a young Polish lady, the daughter of

Colonel Lapuchin, and soon after made his appearance in the National Assembly. The regent for a long time listened with incredulous contempt to the reports which were brought her of Peter's progress; but, being at length convinced of their truth, she began to fear him, and set about a series of long and wicked intrigues designed to compass his death. The intrigues were not successful. After many quarrels between the czar and the regent, the former triumphed, and forced his sister to leave the throne. She went on plotting against him, and he threw her into prison. Peter assumed the reins of government in 1689, when he was but seventeen years of age, giving nominal sovereignty and precedence to Ivan, who was really nothing but a puppet in his hands. Ivan's mock authority ended with his death, in 1696.

Peter had learned from Lefort and Timmermann Russia's deficiency in all that makes the moral and material greatness of a nation, her inferiority in these respects to the other nations of Europe; and his first efforts as czar were given to the creation of an army and a navy. He met with rapid success in the former work, but not in the latter. Nature had not designed

Russia for a great naval power; but Peter determined that she should become such a power in spite of Nature. He enticed skilled engineers to Russia through the promise of liberal rewards, and had many ships built under their direction. Desirous of improving his empire in all respects, he sent many of the young nobles abroad to study the manners and customs of enlightened nations. Others were sent away to learn the art of war. At length, Peter resolved to make a tour himself in quest of information.

He was twenty-four years of age when he set out on his travels. It was at a time when questions of the most vital importance were agitating all Europe, — the era of Louis XIV. of France, of Charles XII. of Sweden, of William the Stadtholder of Holland.

The czar left Russia in the guise of an inferior officer; proceeding through Prussia and Hanover to Amsterdam, where he took miserable lodgings near the dockyard of Saardam, among the fishermen. Assuming the name of Peter Timmermann, he hired out with a ship-builder, working his regular hours, and receiving his wages, like the other workmen: and yet, from his wretched hut at Saardam, he kept an eye on the vast concerns of his empire, then at war with Turkey; issuing orders to the army which resulted in signal victories.

From Holland he went to England, taking up his residence in the dockyards at Deptford, where he was known as "Captain Peter." Many stories are told of his life here, — of the zeal with which he pursued his work and his inquiries. He cared nothing for the moral advancement of his country; but his whole heart was in Russia's material progress. So intense was his thirst for knowledge, that, while examining some old instruments of Papal torture in Holland, he expressed a great desire to see some one broken on the wheel! When he offered one of his own men for that purpose, he could not understand why so reasonable a gratification should be denied him.

From England he went to France; thence to Vienna: he was on the eve of going to Venice to inspect the naval armaments there, when he heard that Sophia had a second time incited the Strelitz to revolt.

Hastening back to Russia in the most ungovernable fury, he took such dire vengeance that the whole empire trembled at mention of his name. He ordered the entire body of the Strelitz to be put to death, and very few escaped the cruel sentence. For five months, the axe, the gibbet, and the wheel were in constant activity in Russia. With his own hand, Peter sometimes performed the office of executioner. One day, with a wine-cup in one hand and an axe in the other, he smote off twenty heads within an hour, — one after every bumper of wine! Having reason to suspect his wife of complicity in the revolt, he gave her the terrible punishment of the knout, and then, having divorced her, banished her to the cloister for life. He had never loved his wife; the marriage had been one of policy; and when, as a member of the old Russian party, she opposed his reforms, and attempted to thwart his plans, a deep hatred against her entered his heart. The Princess Sophia was sentenced to have her head shaved, and be shut up in a convent for life. There she lived under the name Marpha, and died broken-hearted in 1704.

The ruling idea of Peter's life was to make Russia the centre of trade between Europe and

Asia. To attain this end, he must have outlet to the Baltic, and a canal connecting the Dwina and Volga Rivers, thus opening a communication between the northern seas and the Black and Caspian Seas in the south. In pursuance of this plan, he in 1703 laid the foundations of St. Petersburg. The site of the future capital was a vast morass, lying in the midst of pestilential swamps, and situated in a climate of sixty degrees north latitude, with a most rigorous winter lasting eight months of the year. No man but Peter would have dreamed of founding a city in such a place.

Innumerable obstacles, among which was an almost entire lack of building-material, lay in the way; but Peter did not for a moment abandon his purpose; and, before a year, the new city contained thirty thousand houses and huts. A hundred thousand workmen are said to have perished from hardship and exposure that first year. St. Petersburg exists to-day, a city of half a million souls; but its foundations sink as far beneath the earth's surface as its splendid church-spires and palace-domes tower above it, for the whole city is built on piles, and its very existence is a miracle, a triumph of the audacity and power of man over the implacable forces of Nature.

Conquest was not Peter's policy. His aim was to concentrate the powers of government, and civilize the people. He did not, however, think it necessary to civilize or to govern himself. "He gave a polish to his nation," says Voltaire, "and was himself a savage." It has been said of him, that, although the *man* was sometimes deformed by cruelty and drunkenness, the *sovereign* was always great. With all his brutality, he had a taste for science and the fine arts, and earnestly sought their advancement.

In one of Peter's campaigns against Charles XII., among the prisoners of war he had met a young Livonian peasant-girl seventeen years old. She came to one of his generals in tears for the loss of her husband, who had perished in the *mêlée*, and to whom she had been married only the day before. Peter first made her his mistress. In 1707 he privately married her, and for years after publicly acknowledged her as his wife. Upon her marriage and adoption into the Greek Church, her name was changed from Marpha to Catherine.

CATHERINE, 1725-1727,

was remarkable neither for beauty nor talent; but she was, in her youth, graceful in person, and pleasing in manner; she had also great good sense, and a temper so sweet that she alone could quiet the czar in those mad frenzies of passion to which he was subject. Her devotion to Peter was boundless. She accompanied him everywhere, even to scenes of war and danger; and her courage never faltered, even in the most trying hour. It is said that after the battle of Pruth, which was so disastrous to Russia, Catherine, by her genius, her heroism, and her influence over the czar, saved the army and the empire.

Nineteen years after his return from his first journeyings, Peter again set out on his travels; and this time Catherine accompanied him. Although the czar was never ashamed of his peasant-wife, he would not take her to France, and have her subjected to the criticisms of the most polished and heartless court in Europe. He left her behind in Holland.

Peter was received everywhere with the most

profound respect. He knew all the languages of Europe, and, when he chose, could regulate his manners to the strictest rules of etiquette. He visited his old haunts, and that insatiable thirst for knowledge which had prompted his first travels remained with him still. Nothing escaped his observation. On their return, the czar and czarina visited the royal family at Berlin. Frederick of Prussia, and Peter of Russia, had many traits in common, — the same blunt, soldierly qualities, the same contempt, for vanity and luxury. The Prussian queen and princesses were, however, beings of different mould; and we see from the pert letters of the Princess Wilhelmina that Peter and Catherine did not escape criticism at this court. The young princess writes, —

"When Peter approached to embrace my mother (the queen), her Majesty looked as if she would rather be excused. The czar is tall and well-made: his face is handsome; but there is in it a rudeness which inspires dread. He was dressed like a sailor, in a frock without lace or ornament. The czarina is short and lusty, remarkably coarse, and without grace or animation. One need only see her to become satisfied of her ignoble birth. At the first blush you would take her for a German actress. Her clothes look as if bought at a doll-shop, every thing is so old-fashioned, and so bedecked with silver tinsel. She was decorated with a dozen orders, and portraits of saints and relics, which occasioned such a clatter when she walked, you would suppose an ass with bells was approaching."

Peter, who might have formed an alliance with the highest princess of Europe, was always content with his Catherine. Ever anxious to exalt her dignity, he founded the order of Saint Catherine in her honor, and had her publicly crowned empress. When at last, on the 28th of January, 1725, he lay dying in her arms, he made motions to have pen and paper brought him, and with trembling hand wrote out his last commands. "Let every thing be given to"—were the only words that could be deciphered: but Catherine and her party affirmed that it had been the czar's intention to leave the throne to his wife, if she survived him; that, with this end in view, her coronation as empress had taken place in May of the preceding year.

Peter died in the fifty-third year of his age, of

a fever brought on by reckless exposure in the rescue of a boat which had run aground upon the rocks. The only son of his marriage with Catherine having died in early childhood, it was supposed by many that he intended to settle the succession upon Anna Petrowna, his favorite daughter, a beautiful and amiable young princess; but Catherine, with the aid of Menzikoff, seized the government.

Peter the Great will always remain one of the most notable characters of history, — a man of sterling virtues united to glaring faults, and passions so ungovernable that they revive the memory of Ivan the Terrible. The two blackest crimes recorded against him are the murder of the Strelitz, and complicity in the death of Alexis his eldest son, the son of the wife he hated. This son, to whom Peter was always a stern judge rather than a tender parent, had in his earliest years, at his mother's knee, imbibed a spirit of opposition to his father; and when, in manhood, that feeling broke out in open revolt, Alexis was tried, and sentenced to death. Immediately after, he died suddenly, from poison, which few doubted was given at his father's command.

In Peter, a mind strong to do and dare, a will that defied opposition, and a courage that quailed before no danger, were united to herculean strength of body, and a colossal stature of six feet and four inches. Nature had formed him for a ruler of men, and he became their tyrant. "I am the state," he said; "the state is in *me;* all ought to be done for me, the absolute master, who owes to God alone an account of his conduct." "All *for* the people, nothing through them," was his motto. He has been described as a merciless Procrustes, who cut men down to the dimensions of his iron bedstead. He carried out his reforms in the State with an utter disregard to the wishes of the people; and so great were his innovations in the Church, where he abolished the office of patriarch, and took the rule into his own hands, that the priests really thought him Antichrist. But yet to him, more than to all others combined, Russia owes her power and greatness. He reconstructed the empire, reformed its manners and customs, and even changed the national instincts. The title of Czar not seeming to him equal to the dignity of his position, he ordered the synod and senate to proclaim him "Emperor and Autocrat of all the Russias," — a title which has been retained by his successors, although "czar" still remains a familiar and popular epithet for the sovereign. The obsequious senate also added the titles of "The Great," and "Father of his Country."

Catherine reigned two years; and it would have been better for her fame if she had never reigned at all. Menzikoff, her prime-minister and favorite, was really supreme in power. This Menzikoff had risen from the ignoble position of pastry-cook's servant to the highest office within the gift of his sovereign. Peter, a judge of men, had invested him, although he was entirely uneducated, with the highest dignities of the state; and now the concerns of the vast empire Peter had left were in the hands of two persons who could neither read nor write.

The haughty old nobility of the realm could ill brook the sway of two such low-born, illiterate rulers. Menzikoff, who was possessed of great natural ability, cared neither for their scorn nor their hatred; but the contempt, ridicule, and opposition which relentlessly pursued her, sank deep into Catherine's soul, and she sought refuge in dissipation. The virtues which had distinguished her during Peter's lifetime seemed to have deserted her, although that humane disposition, whose influence had often deterred the czar from acts of violence and cruelty, characterized her to the last. She fell into habits of intoxication, which hastened her death at the early age of thirty-eight.

PETER II., 1727-1730.

Soon after the death of Peter the Great, his daughter Anna was married with great pomp to the Duke of Holstein. Catherine had left the empire by will to Peter, the son of the ill-fated Alexis, a lad of eleven years; and had chosen her daughters Anna and Elizabeth, Menzikoff, and six other personages of the court, a council of regency. A second article of her will enjoined a marriage between Peter and the daughter of Prince Menzikoff.

Menzikoff soon managed to obtain the supreme power; but his cruelty and rapacity were so great, that a conspiracy was formed against him; and he with his whole family, including the bride-elect, was banished to Siberia, where they all remained to the end of their days.

Peter II., under the tutelage of the Dalgowky family, one of the most ancient in Russia, reigned two years and nine months, when he died suddenly of small-pox, at the age of sixteen, deeply regretted, for he was a youth of great promise. Even in his short career he performed many acts which endeared him to the people: among them were two which won him great applause from the old conservative party of the realm, — the removal of the capital back to Moscow, and the release of his grandmother from her unjust imprisonment. The charges against this much-persecuted lady were disproved: she was declared the only legitimate wife of Peter the Great; and, loaded with riches and honor, she lived in Moscow to the end of her days.

ANNA, 1730-1740.

The male line of Romanoff became extinct in Peter II.; but the female branch still existed in the persons of three daughters of Ivan, half-brother to Peter the Great. The second of these daughters, Anna, dowager-duchess of Courland, was elected to the throne. She proved an able and warlike princess, adopting Peter I. as her model in policy. Her reign of ten years would have been productive of great blessings to the empire, if she had not been so much under the influence of her prime-minister and favorite, Biren, a bad and criminally-ambitious man.

Anna left the empire, by will, to her great-nephew, Ivan, the grandson of her oldest sister, the Duchess of Mecklenburg, stipulating that Biren should administer the government until the child had attained his seventeenth year. Biren's cruelties were so great, that the people rose in rebellion, and banished him to Siberia, whither he had himself been the means of sending twenty thousand exiles. The infant sovereign was also deposed, and placed in close confinement, which terminated only at his death.

ELIZABETH, 1741-1762,

the youngest daughter of Peter the Great and Catherine, was crowned empress, and ruled for twenty years. She was a woman of narrow, superstitious ideas, of depraved morals, and profound dissimulation. Averse to business, and fond of pleasure, she left state affairs mostly to her ministers. Her one redeeming feature was an aversion to the taking of human life. She vowed that in her reign no culprit should suffer death; but exile, the torture, and the knout — even worse punishments than death — were dealt out with a liberal hand. Elizabeth chose Charles Peter Ulric, the son of her deceased sister Anna, as her successor.

PETER III., 1762,

at the time of his aunt's death, had long been a resident at court, and, sixteen years previously, had married Sophia Augusta of Anhalt-Zerbst, who, upon her adoption into the Greek Church, received the baptismal name of Catherine. She is known to the world as the famous and infamous Catherine the Great.

Peter had grown up under the evil influences of a corrupt court, where his education had been neglected, and his morals perverted; but he possessed many excellent traits of character. Frank, generous, and incapable of malice or revenge, his heart was always better than his head, He carried forward some necessary reforms, but made some very arbitrary innovations both in Church and State. Thoroughly German in all his feelings, his enthusiasm for Frederick the

Great, whom he made his model in most things. amounted nearly to madness.

As Peter was disfigured by small-pox, and possessed of no fascinations either of person or manner, he had excited Catherine's aversion from the first. There had long been entire estrangement between the royal pair, and Catherine knew that Peter was contemplating divorce: she knew, also, that her numerous infidelities had given him abundant cause. A conspiracy against the czar — headed, no doubt, by Catherine and her paramour, Gregory Orloff — resulted in his deposition, and, a week after, in his death by poison. He had reigned only one year.

CATHERINE THE GREAT, 1762-1796.

The conspirators placed Catherine upon the throne, and for thirty-four years she lived to disgrace that ill-won dignity. Of all the bad women of history, unless, perhaps, we except Catherine de Medici, Catherine of Russia seems the worst. She has, to be sure, found her eulogists. She affected an interest in letters, and invited literary men to her court, chief among whom was Voltaire; and they loaded her with flatteries. Frederick the Great used to call her his philosophic sister: an obsequious senate gave her the titles of "The Great," "The Wise," "The Mother of her Country." But we may safely affirm that those who flattered her most, at heart most thoroughly despised her. None can deny her talent, her energy, and her political sagacity; but her ability has been much overrated. She was *really* great only in wickedness.

Bloodthirsty, revengeful, thoroughly selfish, unscrupulously ambitious, a hypocrite, a tyrant, a sensualist, and an atheist, she had the fewest possible redeeming virtues.

Stimulated by vanity to the commencement of great undertakings (few of which she ever finished), to the adoption of foreign customs and maxims of government for which her people were not prepared, waging wars solely for conquest and glory, all that she accomplished was of but small permanent benefit to Russia.

During her whole reign, Catherine was engaged in wars mostly of aggression; and she was never known to hold a treaty sacred when interest demanded that it should be broken. Her sins against the acknowledged laws of nations were numerous and appalling; but the stupendous crime of her reign was the partition of Poland, which she carried out with a persistency and inhumanity far more revolting than that of her allies, Prussia and Austria, and in which she had the lion's share. She also wrested large territories from Turkey. It was her plan to drive the Mohammedans from Europe, and to erect on the dismembered remains of the Turkish Empire a new sovereignty to be given to one of her lovers.

Active in pushing forward so-called reforms when they would redound to her own glory, Catherine cared nothing for the real good of her people: she was capable of no exalted virtue. Self-laudation and self-gratification were her sole earthly aims. She always had money to lavish upon herself and upon her numerous lovers, yet never any to relieve the wants of her oppressed and starving people. We will not dwell upon her character; for the details of her private life form one of the most polluted pages of history.

Catherine is said to have possessed beauty; but it was of that demoniac sort which might have characterized the fallen angels. Her features, although not offensively masculine, were those of an ambitious woman. Rather above the medium height, her carriage was majestic, and she seemed one born to command. She was sprightly in her manner, and, though an atheist at heart, was outwardly devout. She made great literary pretensions, and, among other works, she wrote a history of her times; but her knowledge was superficial, and her works were of so little merit, that they have not been considered worth preserving.

Without a shadow of right to the throne herself, she took good care to remove from her path the true heir, Ivan, who, ever since the beginning of Elizabeth's reign, had been immured in the grim fortress of Schlusselburg. At Catherine's instigation, he was at length assassinated.

There is something inexpressibly mournful in the life of this young prince. From the age of fourteen months to his twenty-fifth year, he was a prisoner. Taught neither to read nor write, allowed none but the lowest associates, knowing nothing of the world beyond his prison-walls, his whole nature became imbruted; and he had almost relapsed into idiocy, when death mercifully came to his relief.

There was another possible claimant to the throne, — a young and beautiful daughter of the Empress Elizabeth, whose only marriage had been a clandestine one to a singer. She lived in the most retired manner at St. Petersburg, where she was being educated under the name of the Princess Tarrakanoff.

Prince Radzivill, indignant at Catherine for the wrongs she was heaping upon Poland, saw in this young girl an instrument of future revenge. Having gained over her guardians, he conveyed her with her governess to Rome.

Catherine took prompt measures toward frustrating his designs. She confiscated his Polish estates, so that his only resource in Rome was the money derived from the sale of his diamonds and other ornaments. These being nearly exhausted, Radzivill set out for Poland, leaving his ward and her governess in extremely reduced circumstances, which he hoped to relieve on his return. Upon his arrival in Poland, Catherine offered to restore his estates if he would bring the young princess back to Russia. He refused to comply with this condition; but, as the price of his restoration to fortune, he promised not to press her claims to the throne.

Alexis, one of the four brothers Orloff, — all of whom were the pliant and remorseless instruments of Catherine's will, — went to Leghorn at command of the empress, and there laid a snare for the young princess. Securing the aid of a base Neapolitan intriguer named Ribas, he sent him to Rome, where the villain introduced himself as an Italian officer who had come to pay his respects to a princess in whose fortunes he felt the deepest interest. The destitution of the young princess appeared to call forth his deepest sympathy; and he offered assistance, which was thankfully received.

Having by these acts fully won the confidence of the unsuspecting child, Ribas declared that he had come, commissioned by Alexis Orloff, to offer her the throne of Russia; that, if she would consent to marry Orloff, he would head an insurrection in her favor.

The young princess had already been informed by Prince Radzivill of her claim to her mother's throne, and the hopes he had fostered now seemed confirmed: so she, with fatal alacrity, yielded to the designs of those who sought her ruin.

When, after a time, Alexis Orloff himself came to Rome, she gave him a joyful welcome; and when, as a part of his carefully-prepared instructions, he declared that he had fallen in love with her, she believed him, and loved him in return; for Orloff, who was still a young, handsome, and fascinating man, was well calculated to enslave the fancy of an inexperienced girl of sixteen. When he asked her hand in marriage, he won a grateful assent.

Feigning a desire to have the marriage performed according to the Greek ritual, Orloff bribed villains to assume the office of priest and witnesses. Soon after the marriage, he told the pretended bride, that, as their stay in Rome exposed them to remark and criticism, their best course would be to repair to some other Italian city, and there await the revolution which was to place her on the throne. They went to Pisa, where Orloff hired a splendid palace, and where he seemed the most tender, devoted, and thoughtful of husbands, accompanying the princess everywhere, and apparently knowing no greater happiness than to gratify her tastes and wishes.

The Russian squadron, under Admiral Gregg,

had entered the port of Leghorn; and Orloff, pretending that urgent business called him to that city, invited the princess to accompany him.

On their arrival in Leghorn, they took apartments provided for them at the house of the English consul. The princess was treated with the utmost respect, ladies of the highest rank paying her marked attention. She found herself courted, flattered, and idolized; and in that brilliant circle, of which she was the centre, it seemed the study of all to secure her some new pleasure. At the theatre, upon the promenade, wherever she appeared, she was the observed and admired of all.

At length the princess, having heard glowing accounts of the splendor of the Russian ships, expressed a desire to visit the fleet. As her slightest wish was equivalent to a command, the request was joyfully granted; and the next day was fixed upon for the visit. Meantime she was assured that every thing should be properly arranged for her reception.

On arriving at the water, she was led to a boat with splendid awnings, where the English consul and several ladies took seats with her. A second boat conveyed Count Orloff and Admiral Gregg; a third, the Russian and English officers.

The boats put off from shore amid the cheers of an immense concourse of people; and the fleet received the august party with music, salvos of artillery, and repeated huzzas. These honors, Orloff assured the princess, were paid to her as heiress to the Russian throne. As her boat came alongside the ship she was to enter, a splendid chair was let down; and, seated in this, she was hoisted on deck.

Scarce had she set foot on the ship when she was handcuffed, and ordered to descend into the hold. Having full faith in her supposed husband, she indignantly appealed to him for protection; but he was deaf to her prayers. She threw herself at his feet, and bathed them with her tears; but tears could not move the man whose life had been one long record of crimes, — the man who had presented the poisoned cup to the Czar Peter at Catherine's command.

The next day, the ship which bore the unhappy Princess Tarrakanoff sailed for Russia. On arriving at St. Petersburg, the princess was immured in a gloomy fortress on the banks of the Neva.

The citizens of Leghorn, who had supposed the princess the lawful wife of Orloff, had in good faith paid her all the honors due to her rank, and were highly indignant at the infamous betrayal she had received in their very midst. The court of Tuscany at once complained of the outrage both to the courts of St. Petersburg and Vienna. Leopold of Austria made a formal protest; other rulers also entered complaints against Orloff: but, upheld by Catherine, he braved unblushingly the resentment of princes and people.

The fate of the unfortunate Princess Tarrakanoff is involved in mystery, though it is generally supposed that she was drowned in the terrible inundation of the Neva which occurred in September of the year 1777. If at that time an inmate of the fortress, she must have perished; for the water rose ten feet, and undermined the walls. It has been affirmed by some that she was murdered in her prison by Catherine's command: others have declared that she escaped into Germany, where she lived and died in the strictest retirement. But the first supposition is probably the true one.

Catherine II. died in 1796.

Voltaire called Catherine II. "the Semiramis of the North." Others have given her a title she more justly deserves, "the Louis XIV. of Russia;" for, both in its strength and weakness, her character was closely allied to that of the vain, pompous, despotic, voluptuous, yet able *grand monarque* of France.

Catherine raised the Russian court to a high degree of splendor; and, although she had reached the sixty-eighth year of her age, she seemed to have had no thought of the time when she must bid adieu to all earthly grandeur, to have made no provision for that one momentous event which comes alike to monarch and to slave. In the height of her power, in the midst of her ambitious dreams, she was suddenly stricken down by apoplexy. Death had come to her without a moment's warning; and the vast empire, whose aggrandizement had been the one dream of her life, must pass to her son Paul, — the son whom from his birth she had hated and persecuted.

PAUL I., 1796-1801.

Peter the Great, by an ukase issued in 1722, had given the Russian sovereign the right of choosing his successor, not limiting the choice even to members of the royal family. It had doubtless been Catherine's intention to exclude her son, and leave the succession to her grandson, Alexander. She had grossly neglected Paul, kept him at a distance from court, and treated him with a more than contemptuous indifference; even taking from him his two eldest sons, that she might herself superintend their education.

Paul had fully returned his mother's hatred; and one of the first acts of his reign was to repeal the ukase of Peter the Great, and restore the succession by hereditary descent to the male line; the crown to devolve upon a woman only when every male heir was extinct. Throughout Paul's brief reign, his policy, if he may be said to have had any policy as czar, was to undo every thing done by his mother.

Catherine had not allowed her husband imperial sepulture: he had been buried in the consecrated ground surrounding the monastery of Saint Alexander-Nevsky. Paul had his father's remains taken from the grave, where they had lain for thirty-five years; and at Catherine's funeral the coffin of her husband was placed beside her own, the two being connected by a true-lover's knot, bearing this inscription: "Divided in life, united in death." The two of Peter's murderers yet living, Alexis Orloff and Prince Baradinsky, were forced to stand on each side of the coffin as chief mourners. The prince nearly fainted; but Orloff exhibited no emotion.

Paul was twice married, — first to a princess of Hesse-Darmstadt, who died early; the second time to Maria of Würtemberg, a princess of rare beauty, talent, and virtue. She became the mother of nine children, — four sons, Alexander, Constantine, Nicholas, and Michael; and five daughters.

There was nothing in Paul to awaken popular love or enthusiasm. "A madman in brain, and a Finn in feature," he came to the throne at forty-two years of age, with no knowledge of the mechanism of government, or of the people over whom he was to rule. Two objects seemed to be uppermost in his mind, — to wreak vengeance on the murderers of his father; to pour contempt on the memory of his mother, by annulling all her enactments. He was not bad at heart; yet, as czar, he made all tremble who approached him.

His eccentricities (which really amounted to insanity), his violence, capriciousness, and unreasoning despotism, soon made him many enemies; and, in the fifth year of his reign, a conspiracy was formed against him at St. Petersburg, headed by some of the most influential men of the empire. The first intention seems to have been to induce the czar to abdicate in favor of his eldest son; but his determined resistance led to his death in a scuffle with the chief conspirators, during which he was strangled.

ALEXANDER I., 1801-1825.

Alexander, who inherited the beauty, grace, and gentle disposition of his mother, ascended the throne at the age of twenty-four. He had been carefully educated at his grandmother's court; the enlightened and conscientious, although free-thinking, Cæsar Laharpe having been his chief tutor. Though he had early imbibed the philosophical principles of Catherine and Frederick the Great, they could not long hold sway over a mind naturally inclined to religious mysticism.

When Alexander came to the throne, the ruling

ideas of Peter the Great had been carried out. The material reformers had had their day: what the empire now most needed was a moral reformer in its czar. The young ruler sought to be such a reformer in the truest sense. Fired by a nobler ambition than Peter the Great or Catherine had ever known, with all the enthusiasm of youth and the courage of inexperience, he set about those moral reforms which alone can give true grandeur to a nation. Striving to forget old animosities at home and abroad, adopting a pacific policy toward foreign nations, he soon won the enviable title of "Prince of Peace." His early reforms were many and great: among them were the abolition of punishment by torture, and the public traffic in human beings. He also abolished the secret Inquisition, which had held such fatal sway during the reign of Paul. The emancipation of the serfs was a measure which lay very near his heart; but Russia was not in his day prepared for that momentous event. He allowed the serfs to purchase with their freedom portions of land to be held in their own right. While doing all in his power to improve the condition of that unfortunate class, he doubtless paved the way for the abolition of serfdom in Russia. He removed many civil and social restraints which had pressed heavily upon the people. But time would fail to tell of his many beneficent and praiseworthy acts.

During his wars with Napoleon, his efforts in behalf of the wounded of all nations were so great, that the Russian Senate proposed to bestow upon him the title of "The Blessed." Declaring that he had done nothing more than his duty, he modestly declined a title any sovereign might be proud to wear.

He aided his excellent mother in establishing those benevolent institutions which have rendered her name so dear to the Russian people; and he showed his zeal for education by instituting or remodelling seven universities, by founding two hundred gymnasiums or normal schools, and two thousand elementary schools. He was zealous in every good work; his heart bled for the woes and sufferings of humanity; and the oppressed millions of Europe began to look to him as their champion and deliverer.

His accession had been hailed with delight throughout the civilized world. The great German poet Klopstock, in an ode celebrating that event, addressed the young emperor as the tutelary angel of the human race ; and the Russians, so long ground down by despotism, greeted the new sovereign and the new era with transports of enthusiasm never before known among a people by nature reticent and grave.

Alexander, animated by the noblest impulses, did his best to realize the hopes of his country and the world. Possessed of all those qualities which win love and admiration, he was the hope and the pride of his people. He was the most amiable of men ; and with his amiable qualities were blended a deep sensibility, a sincere respect for the dignity of human nature, and that tinge of romance and sentiment which lends such charm to youth, all the more potent when, as in his case, it is united to the highest of earthly stations. Of majestic figure and striking personal beauty, there was a seductive grace in his manner and conversation that fascinated all.

But, with all his admirable qualities, he had not the strength of character requisite in a reformer: the gentleness of his disposition constantly stood in his way. To push forward reforms in a country so ignorant, and so wedded to old customs, as Russia, one needed to be made of the sterner stuff of Peter the Great.

Ere long, the theories of youth lost their charm: the glowing ideal ever before the chivalrous, romantic soul of this liberal-minded sovereign of a despotic empire, became more and more difficult of realization. Russia, unprepared for liberal institutions, chose darkness rather than light; and Alexander had a sad awakening from the Utopian dreams of his youth. He found himself pursued by the bitterest opposition and ingratitude; and discouraged at the magnitude of the work he had attempted, at the hostility to reform of the very classes he had sought most to benefit, he at length sank into supineness and melancholy, and grossly neglected the concerns of the empire,— concerns too vast and intricate for a man of his by no means comprehensive intellect. Early in his reign, Alexander cherished a secret determination to abdicate the throne; and he never fully gave up the idea. Soon after his accession, he wrote to Laharpe, "When Providence shall by its blessing have enabled me to raise Russia to the degree of welfare I desire, the first thing I shall do will be to cast aside the burthen of administration, and retire into some quiet corner of Europe, where I may peacefully enjoy the happiness secured for my country." To quote the words of one of his Russian biographers, "Years glided on. The prince who in early youth had dreamed of a private life on the banks of the Rhine had twice crossed that river with the laurel of victory and the olive-branch of peace, and had avenged the destruction of Moscow by the preservation of Paris. Russia was blazing with the glory of her monarch; Europe was proclaiming him her savior. But amid the splendor of all this greatness, the loftiest ever attained by man, Alexander found no happiness upon his throne. The hope of the youth was still lurking in his heart; and he, on several different occasions, sought to realize it."

After having pursued his progressive policy for nearly twenty years, he intrusted the conduct of affairs to his ministers, at the head of whom stood Count Araktchéieff, a representative of the "Old Russian" party, and, as such, opposed to reform. Through means which have never yet been fully understood, he gained almost entire ascendency over the czar; and the many acts of the last years of Alexander's reign, so contrary to his own enlightened views, may be laid to the charge of this man, who had become all-powerful in Russia. Yielding to his counsels, Alexander turned a deaf ear to the appeals of the Greeks, his religious allies and *protégés;* he lent no moral or material aid to that final struggle against Turkey, in which Greece, by the justice of her cause and the heroism of her deeds, won the respect and sympathy of all Christendom.

Alexander joined the coalition against Napoleon in 1805, and was present at the battle of Austerlitz, where the allied armies of Russia and Austria suffered such a disastrous defeat; yet, always given to hero-worship, he soon after became dazzled by the genius and success of the French emperor. So far did his infatuation go, that he entered into Napoleon's plans for conquest, and even wished to give him his sister Catherine in marriage; but the proposed alliance so much desired by both emperors was prevented by the determined opposition of the empress-mother.

Yielding to the all-powerful influence of this

master-mind, Alexander accepted the secret conditions of the Treaty of Tilsit; and on the 7th of July, 1807, the two emperors met on a raft in the river Niemen, — Napoleon as the monarch of the West, Alexander as the sovereign of the East, — and coolly set about dividing Europe and the world between them.

A rupture soon followed, which in 1812 broke out into open hostilities. Alexander joined the great coalition against Napoleon, bringing into the field an army of about nine hundred thousand men.

After the fall of the French emperor, Alexander, believing that, with the vast armies at his command, it was his mission to act as pacificator of Europe, founded, with Austria and Prussia, the celebrated "Holy Alliance," whose ostensible object was to regulate the affairs of Europe on the basis of Christian charity. Alexander was the heart and soul of this alliance, and in its inception he was no doubt sincere; but, always easily influenced by minds stronger than his own, in carrying out its plans he was insidiously led on to adopt the measures of that "supple, tortuous, dark diplomatist of the old system," — Prince de Metternich.

Alexander's religious views had changed. At the time of the burning of Moscow, he professed to have received divine illumination. In a conversation with Bishop Eylart in the year 1818, he said, "I felt a void in my heart, accompanied by a strange presentiment. I went, I came, I sought diversion. The burning of Moscow at last illumined my soul; and the judgments of God, manifested upon our snow-covered battle-fields, filled me with an ardent faith I had never known before. From that moment I learned to know God as he is revealed in the Holy Scriptures; from that moment I began to understand his will and his laws as I do now. The resolution to devote to God alone my glory, my person, and my reign, has since then matured and strengthened within me. From that time I became another man; and to the deliverance of Europe from ruin do I owe my own safety and deliverance."

His piety seems to have been deep and sincere; and so liberal was his faith, that he prayed with equal fervor in Greek, Roman, or Protestant churches.

A lady had exercised a very marked influence

upon his religious life: she was the celebrated Baroness Krudener, who, after a youth of frivolity, had in her mature years embraced a life of holiness, and who, becoming imbued with the doctrines of the Moravian brethren and the ideas of the well-known mystic visionary Stilling, felt that she had received a call to preach the gospel. This lady had also, years before, won a deep influence over the gifted and spiritual Queen Louise of Prussia.

When upon his second visit to Paris, in 1815, Alexander prepared the draft of the Holy Alliance, Madame Krudener was in the city, and is supposed to have had some share in the work.

Alexander said to the priest of Geneva, "I am about to quit France; and I wish, before my departure, to render a public act of thanksgiving to God the Father, Son, and Holy Ghost, and to invite the people to act in obedience to the gospel. I wish the Emperor of Austria and the King of Prussia to join me in this act of adoration, that the people may see us, like the wise men of the East, acknowledging the superior authority of God the Saviour. Beseech God with me to dispose my allies to sign it." With these words the Russian emperor handed to the priest the draft of the Holy Alliance, which was duly signed by the allied sovereigns.

From the time of his father's tragic death, — in which none have ever thought of implicating him, — Alexander's life was imbittered by melancholy. He sometimes tried to throw off this mental depression by taking part in the gayeties of his splendid court, but he more frequently took refuge in religious mysticism. "Seated upon one of the most exalted thrones, Alexander leads the life of an anchorite," wrote one who knew him well. "He enjoys no pleasures: having scarcely reached his mid-career, in the prime of manhood, he leads a solitary and miserable existence," wrote another.

Doubtless one cause of his melancholy was his estrangement from his wife. When her favorite grandson was only seventeen years of age, Catherine II. had brought about a marriage between him and the Princess Elizabeth of Baden, who was a mere child, a year younger than himself, and his equal in grace, beauty, and amiability.

Never was there a lovelier or a more loving

pair; but, as years passed, Elizabeth's place in her husband's heart became filled by another, — her inferior in all save beauty. Elizabeth strove to hide her sorrow from the world, to find solace for her wounded heart in acts of beneficence and charity; but a grief too deep for words or lamentation had entered her soul, and was slowly undermining the sources of her life.

After long years of estrangement, Alexander awoke from his unworthy dream, and, with all the ardor of a first affection, returned to the wife of his youth, who had never for a moment ceased to love him. By the most delicate and affectionate attentions he sought to make her forget the past; and, her health being seriously impaired, he proposed to accompany her to her native land, as the physicians had decided that she must leave Russia. Elizabeth replied to all proposals for change of air and scene, that the wife of the Emperor of Russia must not leave her husband's country to die in a foreign land; and at length the imperial pair concluded to repair to Taganrog, a small town on the Sea of Azof.

Here love and happiness wrought a wonderful transformation in the empress; her health daily improved, and in the charm of her society the emperor forgot the melancholy to which he had been for years a prey. But, before they had been three months at Taganrog, Alexander was seized with a fever produced by the climate, which, in his case, was aggravated by a chronic tendency to erysipelas. Here, on the 1st of December, 1825, in the twenty-fifth year of his reign, died Alexander I., the emperor of fifty millions of people, soothed to the last by the love and care of her to whom his wandering heart had too late returned, — the true, devoted Elizabeth, who might, through all these years, have been the good angel of his life. To her were given his last words of love; to her his dying message, "*I never felt greater inward peace.*" When speech had failed, he motioned her to draw near; and, a few moments before he breathed his last, he tenderly pressed her hand. When all was over, Elizabeth herself closed the dear eyes, and raising the cross above the mute form of him, whom, since the first day of her marriage, she had never ceased to love, embraced and blessed him. "Saviour, forgive all my sins," she prayed: "it is thy will to take my beloved one from me." Then, retiring to her apartment, she gave her tears free vent. Again and again she returned to the side of the departed one, and breathed to Heaven the most fervent prayers for his soul.

Shortly after the death of her husband, Elizabeth wrote this well-known letter to the empress-mother: —

"Mamma, our angel is in heaven, and I still exist upon the earth. Who would have thought that I, feeble and wasted, could have survived him? Mamma, do not abandon me; for I am utterly alone in this world of grief. Our dear departed one wears in death his own benevolent expression: his smile proves to me that he is happy, and that he sees other things than he beheld while he was with us. My only consolation under this irreparable loss is that I shall not long survive him; that I hope to rejoin him soon."

The hope was realized; for, in less than five months, this loveliest, most amiable of princesses was no more. All who gazed upon that white, wasted face, to which the beauty of youth, so early faded, had come back in death, saw there the face of an angel.

"I myself knew that august pair," says the Russian poet Relieff, who was destined soon to wear a martyr's crown. "*He* was charming as hope, *she* delightful as felicity. It seems but yesterday when Catherine adorned their youthful brows with nuptial coronets of roses, soon to be succeeded by diadems. But, alas! all too soon did the Genius of Death crown their pale brows with poppies! What, then, is life?"

Never had a ruler been more beloved than Alexander; never was one more lamented. The whole land seemed stricken dumb by a mighty sorrow, and the awful silence brooding over the nation was broken only by wailings for the dead. As at the death of William of Orange, "*the little children cried in the streets.*" And yet Alexander had not escaped the common lot of sovereigns. Hatred and malignity had pursued him: at the time of his death, his enemies were forming a conspiracy against his life. The plot was revealed to him, and his last hours were imbittered by the ingratitude and treason of those who should have been the firmest supporters of his throne.

The character of Alexander is one offering

many contradictions, but the general judgment concerning him may be summed up in the words of Chateaubriand: "He may, perhaps, often do wrong; but it is ever his desire to do right."

The English author of "Revelations of Russia" says of him, "The character of the Emperor Alexander presents a singular mixture of liberal views, benevolence, and *finesse*, joined to indolent weakness." Rabbe, author of "*L'Histoire d'Alexandre*," pronounces him brilliant, but superficial, an idealist and a theorist, with a mind full of borrowed ideas and disconnected systems.

Napoleon at St. Helena said of him to Count Las Casas, "The Emperor of Russia is infinitely superior: he possesses abilities, grace and information; he is fascinating; but you cannot trust him; he is not sincere, he is a true Greek of the lower empire. He is, or pretends to be, a metaphysician; his faults are those of his education. . . . If I die here, he will be my successor in Europe."

The reader of the history of those times must form his own opinion of the man, who, for twenty-five years, played so momentous a part in the affairs of Europe; who was the soul of the coalition that defeated Napoleon.

The unprejudiced student of his character must believe in the genuineness of his lofty sentiments, in the sincerity of his efforts for the good of his people and the world. A man of great refinement and deep sensibility, of progressive and enlightened ideas, he was called to the rule of a vast, half-savage empire made up of many races, each wedded to its own ideas and traditions. Never did royal philanthropist and reformer mark out for himself a task so difficult as was Alexander's; and may we not well believe that his errors, which were many, were always errors of the head, and not of the heart?

NICHOLAS I., 1825-1855.

The only children of Alexander and Elizabeth, two daughters, had died in infancy; and, at his death, his brother Constantine was heir to the throne. He had three brothers, — Constantine, nearly two years younger than himself, Nicholas nineteen, and Michael twenty-one, years younger. The order of succession being now firmly established in Russia, it was naturally expected that the crown would devolve upon the Grand Duke Constantine. As he was the only one of the three sons of Paul who resembled his father, the prospect of his rule was far from agreeable; but the masses of the Russian people — loyal even to idolatry, and fatalists by birth and education — were prepared to accept meekly and uncomplainingly the sovereign sent them by God.

All of Paul's sons, excepting Constantine, inherited the beauty of their mother. Constantine was uglier even than his father, having the same Calmuck physiognomy in an exaggerated degree. His nose lay flat against his face; thick white brows, always in motion, lent a strange, ferocious expression to his deep-set blue eyes; while the lower part of his face was red, heavy, and uncouth. He had also all the wild turbulence, obstinacy, and eccentricity of the Emperor Paul, while his abilities were far inferior.

Wayward and petulant, and not without a certain kind of quick wit, his oddities as a child had greatly amused his grandmother, Catherine II., while his mother, as is the way with mothers, had petted and fondled, most of all her children, this strange being, who seemed like a changeling in the royal nest.

He hated books, and set his face as a flint against study. "I will not read," he said to one of his tutors: "*you* read; and the more you read, the bigger fool you are." He would learn nothing but military tactics, and these were always his delight. As he grew older, he was extremely fond of drilling soldiers, and was a very martinet in matters of military equipment and discipline, often showing great severity for the slightest breach of soldiery duty or etiquette. "I hate war," he once said, "it so spoils the soldiers' uniforms."

He had real military talent. When only twenty years of age, he distinguished himself in the Italian campaign; and, in token of his approbation, his father gave him the title of Cæsarovitch, of which he was very proud, and which he retained through life. He also showed great bravery at the battle of Austerlitz.

He was not bad at heart; but, when aroused to anger, his outward aspect and demeanor were those of a savage. He showed great reverence for the memory of his father, and was the most tender and respectful of sons to his widowed mother. He cherished a blind idolatry for the imperial dignity, and his brother Alexander was his idol. Content to be a mere cipher by the side of the great czar, so different in all respects from himself, he accompanied him everywhere, showing himself at all times the most loyal and obsequious of subjects. He proved that a tender, sympathetic heart lay beneath the rough exterior by which alone the world knew and judged him, when, in the campaign of 1812, many of the French wounded fell into his hands. If these unfortunate men had been his own brothers, he could not have treated them with greater care or kindness.

In 1815 Alexander confided to him the military government of Poland, and he took up his residence in Warsaw. His rule was tyrannical in the extreme. He shut himself up in his palace, being visible to the people only at military reviews; but he took the greatest interest in the internal prosperity of Poland, and soon learned to love his adopted country better than his own.

Catherine II. in the last year of her life had married Constantine to the Princess Julienne, sister of the late King Leopold of Belgium. The bridegroom was seventeen, the bride fifteen years of age. There was no affection on either side, and, two years after the marriage, the unloving pair separated by mutual consent. The young wife returned to Germany, where, in the enjoyment of a liberal pension and the title of Grand Duchess, she lived to the end of her days. Nothing could ever induce her to return to Russia.

Even Constantine was to have his romance, though it came to him late in life. In the year 1820 he fell desperately in love with Jeanne Gudzinska, a young Polish countess; and, having obtained a divorce from his wife Julienne by imperial ukase, he married Jeanne. This lady, fragile and delicate in constitution, refined in manners, and endowed with every mental and moral charm, exerted a wonderful influence over the rough, eccentric Constantine, whose affections never for a moment swerved from their first and only object. To the last, Constantine treated his wife with the chivalrous devotion and tenderness of a lover. For her sake he resigned the proudest crown on earth.

Jeanne not being of royal birth, the marriage had been, as it is called, by the left hand; and, to gain the emperor's consent to it, Constantine had relinquished his title to the throne. Alexander, knowing that the fantastic character of his brother might revive in the empire the memory of Paul, and perhaps result in a like mournful tragedy, seems to have made this marriage a pretext for carrying out a plan of excluding Constantine from the succession.

The agreement had been secret, being known probably only to the emperor, the empress-mother, and the Grand Duke Nicholas. The act of abdication, duly signed and sealed, had been deposited with the senate, to be opened only after Alexander's death.

Tidings had reached St. Petersburg that the czar, whose illness at Taganrog was well known, was convalescent, and a thanksgiving service was being held in the royal chapel; but, in the midst of the Te Deum, a messenger entered, announcing Alexander's death. The empress-mother fainted; and, on being restored to consciousness, her first words were, "Poor Russia!" She probably distrusted the good faith of Constantine's resignation, and feared a bloody strife between the rival brothers. Nicholas at once ordered a priest to place the gospels and the cross before his mother, and took the oath of allegiance to Constantine, who was that very day proclaimed emperor. Messengers were at once despatched to Warsaw to confer with Constantine; and, after an interregnum of three weeks, written documents came from him, confirming his resignation in 'the most emphatic and solemn manner, and offering loyal allegiance to his brother. Nicholas no longer hesitated, and was immediately proclaimed czar.

Constantine seems never to have regretted his decision. He knew that he was unfit to rule; he knew, also, that his wife — a Roman Catholic in faith, and not of royal birth — could never at court receive the honors due to an empress; that his children would be ineligible to the throne. Loving Poland with all the depth of his really warm nature, supremely happy in a domestic life which had wrought an entire change in his character, he gladly resigned to his younger and more ambitious brother the "glorious fatigues of greatness," the pomps and burdens of a throne.

Nicholas mounted the throne on the steps of a bloody revolution, which shook Russia to its centre. None of the three brothers of Alexander were personally beloved; but Constantine was the favorite of the army, and the army declared for him. Many citizens of the capital joined in the revolt; for it seemed a thing past belief that Constantine had, of his own accord, relinquished the most brilliant throne on earth.

The capital had for years been plotting rebellion, — a rebellion not so much against the person of the czar as against the principle of autocracy; and the supposed usurpation of Nicholas became a pretext for revolt, of which the discontented spirits gladly availed themselves.

Nicholas suppressed the rebellion with great vigor and cruelty. For eighty years, Russia had not beheld an execution; but the new czar restored the death-penalty, and many of the best and bravest of the land perished on the scaffold. Many more were banished to Siberia and the steppes of the Caucasus, — that military Siberia of Russia; and the emperor, years after all occasion for severity had ceased, continued to glut his revenge. The darkest trait in the character of Nicholas was his implacability. He never forgave or forgot an injury.

From the commencement of his reign, he resolved to govern by his absolute will, without being hampered by a constitution. He was an autocrat in the broadest sense of the word. "despotism poured out of his nostrils." The absolute and irresponsible master of more than sixty millions of souls, he soon began to think himself infallible. As years passed on, his character grew hard as steel. He loved Russia with his whole heart, and desired her highest good; but he wanted to reform her in his own way. She must have no will but his; she must never throw off the swaddling-clothes of infancy.

He was a man to project, but not to carry forward, great reforms. His intellect was not of broad range; he had not, like his brother Alexander, been educated for a throne. With all his haughty obstinacy, he was vacillating of purpose. He saw and bewailed the evils of serfdom, but he did not abolish them. Perhaps he dared not: a sense of insecurity, born of the revolution which had ushered in his reign, haunted him continually.

More absolute than even the sovereigns of Persia or Turkey, which have a moral as well as a legislative code in the Koran, he deemed himself the one supreme source from which emanated all power and dignity for his people, — the vicegerent of God on earth.

Chateaubriand says of Alexander I., "While sincere as a man in all that concerned humanity, he was cunning as a demi-Greek in all that related to politics." The words could not apply to Nicholas, whose character was open as the day. He was a tyrant and a despot without the least evasion or concealment.

In a catechism published for Russian children in 1832 by order of Nicholas, and entitled "The Worship that should be rendered the Emperor," we find the following question and answer:—

"How ought want of respect and fidelity toward the emperor to be regarded?"

Ans. "As the most detestable sin, as the most horrible crime."

In another place, this catechism declares that disobedience to the emperor is the same as disobedience to God himself, who will recompense homage and obedience to the emperor in another world, and punish severely and throughout eternity those who may fail to render them.

"As Christ and the apostles meekly submitted to the decree which condemned them to death, so ought we also to know how to suffer and be silent," is another of the precious doctrines Russian priests and parents in this reign were required to teach their children.

Nicholas was possessed of a feverish activity. No man in Russia worked so hard as he. He would rise at four in the morning, and, throwing an old military cloak around his shoulders, set about the herculean task of managing everything, even the minutest details of his vast empire. He wanted to see and hear and know all; he could not endure that any thing should go on without his cognizance. "Not a mouse can stir in Russia without permission from the czar," wrote a traveller of that day.

We need not repeat that oft-told tale of the woes and wrongs he heaped upon Poland. History records no greater crimes than his against that unhappy country. "I will make a Siberia of Poland, and a Poland of Siberia," he declared; and he did his best to verify the words. Up to 1848 he had banished more than sixty thousand Poles to Siberia. Political proscription was followed by religious persecution. The czar was determined that Poland, physically, politically, and spiritually, should be blotted from the map of nations.

By a ukase issued Feb. 14, 1832, the Russian authorities of Poland were ordered to seize upon all male children of the poorer classes, who composed nineteen-twentieths of the inhabitants, and send them to Minsk to be enrolled in battalions, and brought up for the military service of the government. Even in infancy they were torn from parents' arms, from charity-schools and foundling-hospitals, and, under brutal guards of Cossacks, borne by hundreds from their homes, followed often for miles by agonized, imploring mothers. Happy were those who died of hunger and hardship on the way, and thus escaped the untold woes of the life before them. Frederic La Croix, a French writer upon Russia, pronounces this the most atrocious crime in her history, the most atrocious crime in *all* history.

As Nicholas was supreme autocrat of Russia, he sought to be autocrat of Europe. He aspired to rule in the councils of nations, to make the whole world tremble at his power. He was the haughtiest sovereign on earth, and looked with lofty disdain on the lesser potentates around him.

The hereditary ambition of Russia is the absorption of Turkey, and with it the possession of

Constantinople and the Bosphorus, through which alone Russia can hope to become a great maritime power. "I must have the key that unlocks the door of my house," the Czar Alexander said to Napoleon at Tilsit.

Nicholas thought himself powerful enough to carry out this long-cherished enterprise; he had no idea that other nations would dare oppose it. When he found that France and England and Sardinia would unite against him, he still persisted in his purpose. This fatal and obstinate persistency brought on the Crimean war, whose events are familiar to all. The Greek cross was lowered before the crescent. Russia was weakened and humiliated by a series of defeats; and, in the darkest hour of the struggle, the autocrat of all the Russias, a disappointed, almost heart-broken man, lay down to die.

When he felt that his end was near, he said to his son Alexander, "You know that the good of Russia has been the sole end of all my solicitude and all my efforts. I desired to leave the empire fully organized, guaranteed from danger within and without, completely tranquil and happy. God wills otherwise. The burden will be heavy for you." In his last testament he says, "I die filled with ardent love for our glorious Russia, which I have served with all my soul, with faith and with sincerity. I regret that I have not been able to do all the good I so sincerely desired."

No stings of conscience visited the death-bed of the great czar. This man, guilty of so many crimes against humanity, who had caused such unutterable woe to thousands upon thousands of his subjects, died with the heavenly hope and pious resignation of a saint. "I have always prayed for Russia and for you while on earth," he said to his eldest son and heir: "I will pray for you in heaven."

Many virtues adorned the private life of the Emperor Nicholas. His domestic affections were strong and ardent; he was the most devoted of husbands and fathers. Those rigid forms of etiquette upon which he so strenuously insisted in his public life were banished from his family-life. He married at an early age the Princess Charlotte, eldest daughter of William III. of Prussia, and of the "angel good and angel fair," Queen Louise.

This princess, who, upon her baptism into the

Greek Church, received the name of Alexandra Féodorovna, although naturally amiable and pleasing, did not possess her mother's almost angelic loveliness of mind and person. Long residence at the Russian court as the wife of the haughtiest of sovereigns developed in her a distance and superciliousness of manner that did not win hearts. She adored her husband, and her love was fully returned : no happier domestic life could be found in all Russia.

There were seven children in the royal household, — four sons and three daughters, — all inheriting the fine physical traits of both parents. "The royal family of Russia is the handsomest family that ever lived," wrote one who saw these children in their blossoming time. One daughter, Olga, who became Queen of Würtemberg, was ideally beautiful. The Emperor Nicholas in his prime was considered the handsomest man in Europe. The emperor was very proud of his family, and loved his wife and children with an ardor partly due to natural affection, but yet full of that unbounded egotism which adored all in any way united to himself by ties of kindred.

He liked to have his entire family, children

and grandchildren, around him. When his daughter Marie, who had married a son of Eugène Beauharnais, was left a widow with five children, they all came to live at the royal palace, and were treated with the tenderest affection.

Constantine, the second son of Nicholas, was "a faithful copy of his sire." Alexander was cast in a gentler mould, and his father had many misgivings as to his being possessed of those stern qualities which he himself deemed indispensable in a czar of Russia. Knowing that Constantine would be sure to carry out his own policy, Nicholas at one time seriously contemplated choosing him heir. However unlawful such a proceeding might be, it would be allowed to the autocrat of Russia, who was above all law. These two brothers, who were entirely dissimilar in character, never lived amicably together; Constantine always wanted to dictate, and he expected Alexander to obey. Constantine is now President of the Council of the Empire.

ALEXANDER II., 1855-.

At twenty years of age, Alexander set out to visit the different courts of Europe. He is thus described by the Marquis de Custine: —

"I had been told by Russian travellers that the beauty of the heir was a phenomenon, and it is really very striking. He has an agreeable figure and a noble bearing. His complexion is pale; there is an expression of melancholy in his eyes; he evidently suffers. His gracious mouth is not without sweetness; his Greek profile recalls the antique medallions and the portraits of the Empress Catherine. He has a melodious voice, rare in his family, — a gift he has received from his mother. His stature is tall, — too tall for so young a man: he reminds one of his uncle, the Emperor Alexander, at the same age. His air is modest, without timidity; he impresses you as a perfectly educated man. If he ever rules, he will make himself obeyed by love rather than fear."

This young grand duke, like his sons, the Grand Dukes Alexis and Sergius, who have been so recently our country's honored guests, charmed all by the amenity of his manners. While his father won only respect and awe, he won hearts. He had a poetic soul: the well-known poet Joukowsky, the Lamartine of Russia, had assisted in his education.

And yet this prince, at the height of worldly fortune, and with such a splendid destiny before him, was devoured by a secret melancholy. The Russian court in Nicholas' day was far from being a cheerful place; and it is possible that the czar, whose ideas differed so widely in all things from those of his son, had crushed that sensitive soul by his sternness and exactions. At the early age of sixteen, the age when the Russian heir to the throne attains his majority, he had been placed in command of a corps of soldiers, and constant military exercise had seriously impaired his health.

The young heir was melancholy; this fact was evident to all. The czar decided that he should travel, and, while visiting at foreign courts, choose for himself a wife.

The author of "*Souvenirs Personnels de l'Empereur Alexandre II.*" says that the young heir went from court to court. The quest upon which his father had sent him was well known: he received everywhere the warmest greetings and the most flattering attentions. At length he appeared at Hesse-Darmstadt. The Grand Duke Louis had several fair daughters, neither of whom would be likely to say him nay; but he was apparently on the point of leaving this court, fancy-free, as he had left all the others, when, to the great surprise of the ducal family, he asked the hand of the youngest daughter, Marie, in marriage.

This young girl — who was modest, timid, and retiring — was slighted by her more brilliant sisters, and almost ignored by her father. She had not dreamed of fascinating the royal visitor. While her sisters had been decked out in jewels and gorgeous array, she had sat apart in her simple white dress, unheeded, but finding her solace in intellectual and artistic pursuits. "It was the very charm of this reserve, this poetry of isolation, that attracted the notice of Alexander: in the resigned melancholy of this young soul he found an echo of his own." Marie, however, had other attractions; she was lovely in face and form, and possessed an elevated and cultivated mind.

No Russian grand duke could marry a wife outside the pale of his church without forfeiting his birthright: Marie, therefore, went to Russia to study the language, and be baptized into the faith of her future husband. Catholic princesses will not abjure their faith even to obtain a crown: Protestant princesses have more elastic consciences, and the Russian emperors have, thus far, married Protestant wives. The nuptials of Alexander and Marie were celebrated with great pomp on the 16th of April, 1841.

The Empress Marie-Alexandrovna still lives, adding new lustre to the Russian throne by her graces, her virtues, and her intellect. She is represented as a woman of exquisite refinement and culture, as well-informed and progressive, and in full sympathy with her husband's plans for the improvement of his people.

The happy domestic life of the Russian royal family was saddened in 1865 by the death of the heir-apparent, a young man of great promise, who died at the age of twenty-two. He was betrothed to the Princess Dagmar of Denmark. She has since married the present heir; and they have a son who will one day, if he lives, succeed to the Russian throne.

Alexander II. has five sons living,— Alexander, Vladimir, Alexis, Sergius, and Paul,— and a daughter, who is the wife of Queen Victoria's second son, the Duke of Edinburgh.

The Russian emperor is now in the twenty-third year of his reign, and the sixtieth of his age. His first concern upon attaining the throne was to bring the Crimean war, which he had always opposed, to a speedy end. He gained his purpose at the cost of some humiliating but unavoidable concessions to the allied powers. He has not abandoned Russia's ancient policy of territorial extension, but his efforts have been mainly directed to the improvement of his empire.

The grandest achievement of his reign, the grandest ever achieved by any sovereign, is the emancipation of the serfs. He abolished serfdom throughout Russia by imperial ukase in 1861, and throughout Poland in 1864, carrying out the measure in defiance of the bitterest opposition, showing a courage and a persistency equal to that of Nicholas. Thirty millions of people now thank the Czar Alexander II. for deliverance from a thraldom which had endured for two centuries and a half.

Alexander II. has instituted and carried through other great reforms. He has fostered learning and art; he has encouraged the construction of railways and lines of telegraph throughout his empire, and has in every way sought to promote the moral and material happiness of his people. While he has not granted entire religious freedom, or liberty of the press, he has done away with many of the restrictions which pressed so heavily in his father's reign.

Russia is always unjust to Poland; and, although the present emperor has expressed much sympathy for her patriotism and her sufferings, his Polish policy has been the one great injustice of his reign. He suppressed the insurrection of 1863-64 with great severity, and he has emphatically warned this humiliated but heroic people to cherish no further ideas of national independence. He has, however, introduced some of his greatest reforms into Poland; and, if she can be content to remain a Russian province, she has nothing to fear at his hands.

The atrocities committed by the Turks in 1876 on the Christians of Servia and Bulgaria produced intense excitement in Russia, and caused protests and threats from the emperor, who, as the champion of the Greek Church, demanded protection for the Servian and Bulgarian Christians. The several steps in the diplomatic game — played by Russians, Turks, English, Germans, Austrians, and French — which preceded the present war are well known.

Whatever pretexts for this war either side may give, the world knows that it is the hereditary contest for supremacy on the Bosphorus again renewed. "The power which possesses Constantinople must be mistress of the world" is a saying old as Napoleon I., and attributed to him. Both Russia and Turkey appear to believe its truth.

On the 24th of April the emperor issued his manifesto, of which these are the concluding words: —

"Having exhausted pacific efforts, we are compelled by the haughty obstinacy of the Porte to proceed to more decisive acts, feeling that equity and our own dignity enjoin it. By her refusal, Turkey places us under the necessity of having recourse to arms. Profoundly convinced of the justice of our cause, and humbly committing ourselves to the grace and help of the Most

High, we make known to our faithful subjects that the moment foreseen, when we pronounced words to which all Russia responded with complete unanimity, has now arrived. . . . And now, invoking the blessing of God upon our valiant armies, we give them the order to cross the Turkish frontier."

Fifty thousand Russians crossed the frontier that day. The war already begun involves only Russia and Turkey now; but there are national fears, ambitions, and jealousies, hardly concealed at present, which may easily kindle into a war-flame throughout all Europe, and, with religious fanaticism aroused, may draw a large part of Asia into the conflict.

www.ingramcontent.com/pod-product-compliance
Lightning Source LLC
Chambersburg PA
CBHW020121170426
43199CB00009B/589